Samuel Butler
Revised Edition

Twayne's English Authors Series

Herbert Sussman, Editor
Northeastern University

TEAS 2

SAMUEL BUTLER, March 1888.
Photo courtesy of the Chapin Library, Williams College.

Samuel Butler

Revised Edition

By Lee E. Holt

American International College

Twayne Publishers
A Division of G. K. Hall & Co.

Samuel Butler, Revised Edition

Lee E. Holt

Copyright 1989 by G.K. Hall & Co.
Published by Twayne Publishers
A Division of G.K. Hall & Co.
70 Lincoln Street
Boston, Massachusetts 02111

First edition © 1964 by Twayne Publishers, Inc.

Copyediting supervised by Barbara Sutton
Book production by Gabrielle B. McDonald
Book design by Barbara Anderson

Typeset in 11 pt. Garamond
By Williams Press, Inc. of Albany, New York

Printed on permanent/durable acid-free paper
and bound in the United States of America

Library of Congress Cataloging-in-Publication Data

Holt, Lee E. (Lee Elbert), 1912–
    Samuel Butler / by Lee E. Holt.—Rev. ed.
        p.   cm.—(Twayne's English authors series; TEAS 2)
    Bibliography: p
    Includes index.
    ISBN 0-8057-6974-9 (alk. paper)
    1. Butler, Samuel, 1835–1902—Criticism and interpretation.
I. Title.   II. Series.
PR4349.B7Z77 1989
828'.809—dc19   88-31271
                                                                                      CIP

Contents

About the Author

Lee E. Holt was born in Ann Arbor, Michigan, in 1912, and in 1934 he was graduated with high honors from Swarthmore College, having majored in philosophy with minors in German and English. He received his M.A. from Columbia University and his Ph.D. from the University of Wisconsin (1940), where he wrote his thesis on Samuel Butler, examining the critical reception of Butler's books in hundreds of reviews and articles. Professor Holt has held teaching posts at the University of Wisconsin, Indiana University, Union College, and Williams College before going to American International College in Springfield, Massachusetts. Former managing editor of the *CEA Critic,* Holt has published articles on Butler in *Publications of the Modern Language Association, Journal of English Literary History,* the *Papers of the Bibliographical Society of America, English Fiction in Transition,* and the *Samuel Butler Newsletter.* He wrote the article on Butler in volume 18 of the *Dictionary of Literary Biography.* Now retired, Professor Holt lives in Amherst, Massachusetts.

Preface

This book is not a biography of Samuel Butler—biographical studies are abundant, ranging from Henry Festing Jones's two volumes through Malcolm Muggeridge's acid study to the competent biography by Philip Henderson. Rather, it is a critical summary of Butler's work and an evaluation of its worth. It is directed to the reader who wishes to know what Butler thought, not how he lived. Since several of his best books are not now generally available, fairly extensive use of quoted passages has seemed advisable to give the true flavor of his writing. Also more space is devoted to summarizing what he wrote than would have been necessary if all his works were better known.

It is impossible, though, to understand Butler's original and stimulating ideas without paying some attention to the man who thought them. I have based my study on certain psychological deductions regarding the genesis of his originality. These deductions seem to me to be forced upon anyone who dwells for any length of time on his variegated creative activity, even though some of them, since they have not been consistently worked out before, may appear rather novel in Butler criticism. One is forced inevitably when working with Butler to try to understand why he challenged his age in the way he did, why he assailed smugness and blind professionalism yet admired almost to idolatry men who are competent and at home in the world. No critical study should ignore these inevitable questions.

Since this study first appeared in 1964 much important work has been done on Butler. In this revision I have used as much of the recent work as I could, particularly the studies by Avrom Fleishman, Thomas L. Jeffers, U. C. Knoepflmacher, Hans-Peter Breuer, Herbert L. Sussman, Frank M. Turner, and the editorial work of Daniel F. Howard. I express my gratitude to the Chapin Library, Williamstown, Massachusetts, for letting me use its very complete collection of Butler material; to Wayne G. Hammond of the library staff for his help in obtaining the frontispiece for this volume and for checking important details of my text; and to James A. Donovan, Jr., and Wayne G. Hammond for the *Samuel Butler Newsletter* (1978–1988), now unfortunately discontinued. I also express my deep gratitude to Herbert Sussman whose indefatigable editorial work has made this revision much better than it would otherwise have been and to the late Harold C. Goddard of Swarthmore College who first aroused my interest in Butler in his 1933 honors seminar in modern literature.

Lee E. Holt

American International College

Chronology

1879   *Evolution Old and New.* Articles in the *Examiner.*

1880   *Unconscious Memory.*

1881   *Alps and Sanctuaries of Piedmont and the Canton Ticino.*

1882   New edition of *Evolution Old and New.*

1884   *Selections from Previous Works.*

1885   *Gavottes, Minuets, Fugues and Other Short Pieces for the Piano.*

1886   *Luck, or Cunning, as the Main Means of Organic Modification?*

1888   *Ex Voto. Narcissus: a Cantata in the Handelian Form.* Articles in the *Universal Review.*

1893   "L'Origine Siciliana dell' Odissea" and "On the Trapanese Origin of the Odyssey."

1894   *Ex Voto* in Italian translation.

1896   *The Life and Letters of Dr. Samuel Butler.*

1897   *The Authoress of the Odyssey.*

1898   *The Iliad Rendered into English Prose.*

1899   *Shakespeare's Sonnets Reconsidered and in Part Rearranged.*

1900   *The Odyssey Rendered into English Prose.*

1901   *Erewhon Revisited.* Revised edition of *Erewhon.*

1902   Dies 18 June.

1903   *The Way of All Flesh.*

1912   *The Note-Books of Samuel Butler.*

1923–1926   *The Shrewsbury Edition of the Works of Samuel Butler.*

Chapter One
Beginnings

Among the sterling qualities of the work of Samuel Butler are its ability to raise questions; its capacity to give pleasure with its lucid, humorous, vivid prose; and its power to challenge us to greater honesty with ourselves. It demands so much candor and openness of the reader that not everyone can rise to meet it—certainly, most of Butler's contemporaries could not. This man, who once herded sheep in New Zealand and who was also a painter, composer of music, satirist, novelist, art critic, science writer, classicist, poet, and journalist, lived away from publicity and fame and devoted himself to preparing a literary feast.

Why did he do so?[1] Surely not merely, as he humorously suggested, that he might have something to read in his old age! Moreover, his background does not explain his achievements. Many a man has refused, like Butler, to follow the path his father marked out for him, but for most of them nothing has come of this rebellion. Butler, however, rejected not only his father but also many of the stereotypes of his own age; and, unlike other rebels, he created a world of ideas. We shall endeavor to discover what led him to strike out on his very original career and what his discoveries were.[2]

Of course Butler made renunciations to achieve what he wanted to achieve—such is the requirement of life. But the significant fact is that he found sufficient security to dispense with the fear of "giving himself away." His "incarnate bachelorhood,"[3] his carefully organized life, the areas of thought and feeling to which he could not trust himself—all these were bulwarks against the inner originality that he had to control and to channel in order to save himself. A passage in *Life and Habit,* which Butler tells us embodies the original idea for that book and which came to him as he listened to the bells in Montreal,[4] gives a clue to the problem of achieving the unity in diversity for which he strove, and which he saw as the ideal for all human beings:

His past selves are living in unruly hordes within him at this moment and overmastering him. "Do this, this, this, which we too have done, and found our profit in it," cry the souls of his forefathers within him. Faint are the

1

far ones, coming and going as the sound of bells wafted on to a high mountain; loud and clear are the near ones, urgent as an alarm of fire. "Withhold," cry some. "Go on boldly," cry others. "Me, me, me, revert hitherward, my descendant," shouts one as it were from some high vantage-ground over the heads of the clamorous multitude. "Nay, but me, me, me," echoes another; and our former selves fight within us and wrangle for our possession. (43)[5]

Some critics have accused Butler of lacking the tragic sense of life;[6] rather, it might be said that tragedy not in its well understood classical sense but in some new, not yet comprehended shape, was so near him that he had to be systematic, even petty on occasion, to keep it at bay. Excessively orderly people sometimes shield a chaos within. Butler's neat conformity in later years to the gentlemanly life protected his right to risk his all on his unrecognized, unacclaimed odyssey of creation. His possessiveness, his need to relate everything to his own ego, which P. N. Furbank has so effectively pointed out,[7] may have sprung—as it seems to have done with Beethoven[8] and many others—from the necessity of preserving himself from the incursions of originality. It might also be the result of his firm refusal to accede to conventional standards of judgment, though being careful not to outrage them too much, of his conviction that our primary responsibility is to know what our real selves want. He was brewing a heady mixture in his vats. Thus he had to exercise a meticulous control made up of fastidious notebook entries and of careful relations with people, things, money, and emotions; he had to keep the unknown from overwhelming him; instead, he had to turn it into a kind of curative art for mankind. That through him so much of the unknown did turn into curative art is a measure of his success.

Twentieth-century readers of Butler should remember the rules under which upper middle-class English families lived in the nineteenth century: we forget that Samuel Butler was not free to enter any profession he wished, and as eldest son he had more of a claim on the family wealth than we would take for granted. His grandfather had left him a revisionary interest in an estate near Shrewsbury. Both these rules caused monumental troubles and misunderstandings for which he was certainly not much to blame.

Henry Festing Jones traces the Butler family tree back to 1580 and reveals a whole pattern of surrounding figures to whom Butler could relate and of whom he remained always highly conscious.[9] "Stone

House" in Kenilworth, which stayed in the family until 1891, had been lived in by descendants of an eighteenth-century Samuel Butler who was the steward to Lord Clarendon and Lord Leigh; there was a James Butler, surgeon, engineer, artist, who traveled widely and died in the East Indies; then there was Dr. Samuel Butler, headmaster of Shrewsbury, Bishop of Lichfield, and grandfather of our Butler. Butler's life was lived with his father, his mother, his two sisters, his brother Thomas, and a host of other relatives close and distant. He did indeed make fun of these relatives in conversation with his cronies, Miss Savage and Henry Festing Jones, and in his writing; but he also was most kind to them in his letters, in his careful observance of punctilio, and in his calls upon them. He did not publish *The Way of All Flesh* during his lifetime, in part because he desired to spare their feelings.[10]

It seems clear, however, that there must be much truth to the horrendous account of oppression of son by father presented in that work. Ralf Norrman seeks an explanation for Butler's inveterate use of chiasmus (inverting the order AB into BA), of confusing ends and beginnings, right and left, and his deep-seated dualism, and I think correctly finds it in the beatings and terrorism of his earliest youth.[11] Butler himself meditates on his bad relations with his father:

He never liked me, nor I him; from my earliest recollections I can call to mind no time when I did not fear him and dislike him; over and over again I have relented towards him and said to myself that he was a good fellow after all; but I had hardly done so when he would go for me in some way or other which soured me again. . . . An unkind fate never threw two men together who were more naturally uncongenial than my father and myself.[12]

We can verify all this if we read the family letters[13] and note the father's vacillation in money matters, his consistent failure to praise any of his son's accomplishments, even though he might have been man enough to recognize Butler's considerable financial success in New Zealand, and his refusal even to read any of his son's books except his first one. Butler's failure to relate successfully to many of the people in his life, particularly to have a happy and rewarding sex life, can surely be traced to his childhood suffering.

The seeds of revolt sprouted in Butler in spite of himself. In part they grew as a protest against cruelty and against the tyranny of parents over children, of profession over vocation, of the straitjacket of formal life. Mrs. R. S. Garnett and others have viewed Butler's rebellion as unwarranted;[14] one critic describes Victorian family life as the happiest on record.[15] Both miss the point. Butler was not so much excoriating his own family life, or the life of an age—however much he drew on both for the details of his rebellion—as he was defending the principle of freedom. He was crying out in outrage over the maiming wounds inflicted by all insensitivity, all tyranny, all intellectual dogmatism. That he cried out because he had felt these things himself or because they were particularly Victorian is beside the point.

Early Years and Early Writing

The rebellion in Butler seems to have started early and to have grown apace. Yet he seems to have progressed well enough as a student at Shrewsbury and at Cambridge though, like Thoreau, he later accused the universities of teaching nothing of importance. In *Alps and Sanctuaries* Butler says: "I was very happy at Cambridge. . . . I shall ever retain a most kindly recollection both of Cambridge and of the school where I passed my boyhood; but I feel . . . that I have spent as much of my maturer years in unlearning as in learning" (134). Ruth Gounelas tells us that the Cambridge of Butler's day was particularly successful in teaching undergraduates to seek out a middle ground in every controversy.[16] Yet again, like Thoreau, he made excellent use of what he learned, particularly of the classics, the "hypothetical language" of Erewhon. His father had thrashed Latin grammar into him, beginning when he was four, until he knew all the rules by heart,[17] and he graduated from Cambridge twelfth in the Classical Tripos in 1858.[18] Also at Cambridge he wrote for the first time for publication: the *Eagle*, a magazine "written and edited by members of St. John's College, Cambridge" (*A First Year* . . . , 3), printed his two essays, "On English Composition and Other Matters" and "Our Tour."

In the piece on composition he states a conviction that stuck with him and influenced his own writing: "the style of our authors of a couple of hundred years ago was more terse and masculine than that of those of the present day, possessing both more of the graphic element, and more vigour, straightforwardness, and conciseness." He then adds: "a man should be clear of his meaning before he endeavours to give it any kind of utterance, and . . . having made up his mind what to say, the less thought he takes how to say it, more than briefly, pointedly, and plainly, the better" (3). Here is his first move toward independence;

at the start of his career he rejects the style of his age. And he was right to do so. Butler in his best passages achieves a clarity and succinctness most unvictorian. Also, he refuses to find the process of expression mysterious, though it should be noted that to write "briefly, pointedly, and plainly" is not so easy as he implies. Butler's own painstaking and continual revisions of the materials for his notebooks testify to this difficulty. Nevertheless, he remained a lifelong enemy of "fine writing."

Butler had visited Italy, the country which was to mean so much to him, with his family in 1843 and 1853; in 1857 he went there again with a college friend, and his account of this brief trip was his second publication in the *Eagle*. "Our Tour" reflects the high spirits of a youthful excursion. A passage in it involving a memory from his earlier tour is especially meaningful for one who was to expend so much effort crossing boundaries. The passage describes a crossing through a tunnel from one side of a mountain range to the other: "All was the same [as on his present trip]—bitter cold, dense fog, and ever silently increasing hoar-frost: but on emerging from it [the tunnel], the whole scene was completely changed; the air was clear, the sun shining brightly, no hoar-frost and only a few patches of fast melting snow . . ." (11). As we read this we think of the hero of *Erewhon* crossing the range into his unknown kingdom. Even more, we think of the concluding passage of chapter 28, "The Escape": "the light of the afternoon sun welcomes him as he leaves the tunnel, and behold a smiling valley—a babbling brook, a village with tall belfries, and meadows of brilliant green—these are the things which greet him, and he smiles to himself as the terror passes away.[19]

Canon Joseph McCormick, who knew Butler well at Cambridge, kept some short sketches Butler wrote while an undergraduate; these eleven pieces—published in the Shrewsbury Edition of *A First Year in Canterbury Settlement*—again reveal the good spirits and humor of their author. One is a satire on translations, supposedly from Herodotus: "In this way then the Johnians, I say, practise their tub" (28); another, also satirizing translation style, presents scenes from Cambridge to be added to the world view inscribed on Achilles' shield: college buildings, Market Square, two quarreling cricket umpires, a boat race on the Cam; a third describes the methods to be used to create friction and disunion among friends, ways "of producing, fostering, and invigorating strife of all kinds, whereby the society of man will be profited much" (31). Some will remark that Butler spent his life trying to carry out this youthful proposal! Then there is the ironic advice of a father to his son about how to achieve power in the world—put love of self above all else. There is also the typical takeoff on Latin in a skit describing Thomas Bridges's application for the position of shoeblack, followed by the qualifying examinations the authorities set him: "Prove that the shoe may be represented by an equation of the fifth degree. Find the equation to a man blacking a shoe: (1) in rectangular co-ordinates; (2) in polar co-ordinates," etc. (43). In addition there is a humorous description in verse of two deans and a brief drama in which the deans, after complimenting Butler for his piety, are shocked to see him cross the courtyard without gown or cap, bearing a cup, a bottle of cider, lemons, nutmegs, and sugar (49).

It is hard today to believe that as recently as 1854–58 Butler, a Cambridge student, had "never met any one who entertained a doubt" of the Christian miracles.[20] Yet Butler himself suggests that this was so (*Collected Essays*, I, 55).[21] Since he was intending to enter the ministry, however, he was thinking about religion, as is evidenced by a broadside he wrote spoofing the evangelical Simeonites. This broadside may have been placed in the Simeonites' mailboxes, as was the one written by Ernest Pontifex. It is scornful of those who take religion too seriously, and it reflects the conflict in the Church of England between the High Church and the Evangelical parties. It also suggests Butler's lifelong suspicion of zealotry. "Men are disgusted with religion," it concludes, "if it is placed before them at unseasonable times, in unseasonable places, and clothed in a most unseemly dress. . . . A whited sepulchre . . . is an acknowledged humbug, and most of the Sims are not, in my opinion, very far different" (*A First Year* . . . , 59).

Jones tells us that, in preparing for ordination, Butler attempted to ascertain his own reasons for being a Christian.[22] He made a close study of the New Testament in Greek and of the commentators on it; he also worked in London after his graduation as an amateur lay assistant among the poor. When he found, however, that there was no distinction in conduct and character between the boys in his evening class who had been baptized and those who had not,[23] his faith in dogma was destroyed,[24] and he decided not to be ordained. The emphasis given this experience in various of Butler's books suggests that it was no doubt in part a rationalization of a deeper revolt. But it carried much conviction in the nineteenth century.

The shock to Butler of coming to reject the literalism of his parents' religious beliefs together with the fight that ensued about his ordination and future occupation certainly helps to explain his turning everything upside down as he was thus himself turned upside down, though this specific upsetting event was obviously only the culmination of years of differences with his father. He was alienating himself from the world of established verities. No wonder he felt like a lamb that has lost its way, as described in a passage from *Erewhon* quoted by Norrman to illustrate Butler's lostness:

I am there now, as I write; I fancy that I can see the downs, the huts, the plain, and the river-bed—that torrent pathway of desolation, with its distant roar of waters. Oh, wonderful! wonderful! so lonely and so solemn, with the sad grey clouds above, and no sound save a lost lamb bleating upon the mountain side, as though its little heart were breaking. Then there comes some lean and withered old ewe, with deep gruff voice and unlovely aspect, trotting back from the seductive pasture; now she examines this gully, and now that, and now she stands listening with uplifted head, that she may hear the distant wailing and obey it. Aha! they see, and rush towards each other. Alas! they are both mistaken; the ewe is not the lamb's ewe, they are neither kin nor kind to one another, and part in coldness. Each must cry louder, and wander farther yet; may luck be with them both that they may find their own at nightfall (5).

When Butler announced his decision not to be ordained, his father immediately wrote to him threatening to cut off all financial support unless he reconsider, enter the bar, or become a schoolmaster.[25] Butler, however, for reasons not clear, had already set his heart on being an artist. He had begun to take art lessons and was working diligently. Nevertheless, he offered to compromise by studying medicine, by emigrating, or by becoming a farmer in England. His father said no to these suggestions. Samuel then announced his intention of getting along without further parental support. "I have duties to myself to perform," he wrote, "even more binding on me than those to my parents."[26] But he begged for continuing friendship with his family: "I should be very sorry to think that any other connection than the money connection should cease," he wrote, and "I trust . . . that I shall be allowed to correspond with Langar [his family's home]."[27] He refused to make his life "a lie and a sham"[28] by entering a profession he did not believe in simply to please his parents and to win their support.

We find no clear clue concerning Butler's choice of painting as a career. Perhaps he remembered his joy at visiting the galleries in France and Italy, but he never said so. One wonders why he failed at this time to choose either music or literature as a career, certainly as likely as art to arouse his father's opposition, if that was his hidden aim. He had already shown his interest in writing by contributing to the college magazine. He had already taken piano lessons for many years and continued them at Cambridge.[29] Even in his frontier days in New Zealand he entertained visitors by playing Handel to them.[30] He continued to play all his life and later seriously studied musical theory and composed "in the style of Handel." His love of music, particularly of Handel, became an obsession. In 1883 he wrote: "Of all dead men Handel has had the largest place in my thoughts. In fact, I should say that he and his music have been the central fact in my life ever since I was old enough to know of the existence of either music or life. All day long—whether I am writing or painting or walking—but always— I have his music in my head."[31]

The matter of Butler's choice of profession was finally settled by compromise: he temporarily gave up his plan to study art, and his father paid his passage to New Zealand and promised him a sum of £5,200 to get himself established, of which eventually, after some further misunderstandings, £4,200 was paid.[32] On the night of his departure, Butler for the first time in his life did not say his prayers. He never said them again.[33] During the voyage he read Gibbon, a writer notorious in Victorian days for his cynical account of the early development of Christianity.[34]

A New Freedom

The years 1860–64, spent in New Zealand, which is near the 180th meridian, thus upside down from England, were crucial in tempering Butler's nature. On his own in a new environment, he could rub shoulders with all kinds of people; and he could find out how to manage a considerable sum of money and a special kind of industry— sheep raising—so as to come out ahead. When he left New Zealand he had increased his capital to £8,200.[35]

Butler's life in New Zealand has been studied in detail.[36] He showed great energy in exploring the back country for possible pastureland, dealt firmly and successfully with the frontier men opening up the recently colonized territory, and made many good friends. He wrote long letters home that reflect his newfound sense of freedom and independence. The outdoor life led to a vast improvement in his health and contributed to the store of physical energy that was characteristic of him for the rest of his life. Butler might well have been a happier man had he stayed on in New Zealand among friends rather than returning to London to live the circumscribed life he there adopted. But a vague creative longing urged him on.

A First Year in Canterbury Settlement

Butler's first book was actually privately published by the father who had made so much trouble for him and was still making difficulties about giving him all the capital he had promised. After carefully editing Butler's letters home, he combined them with two articles his son had sent to Cambridge for publication in the *Eagle*,[37] wrote a brief preface, and had the whole printed under the title *A First Year in Canterbury Settlement* (1863). Although it appears that Butler himself never liked this book,[38] and had little to do with preparing it for the press, it makes lively reading. Written in a clear, narrative style and full of detailed accounts of the problems faced by the settlers in New Zealand, *A First Year* has a freshness and nonintrospective happiness that smack of the new world. It also has the bragging tone of self-justification, since the letters on which it is based were written home to show a doubting father that his son could succeed.[39] But above all, it remains an interesting record of early days of exploration and settlement of new lands. In addition, it is Butler's first venture into private publication, this time instigated by his father, but later undertaken over and over again by himself.

When reading Butler's later books, it is well to remember that he got his start in a frontier society where each person was expected to stand up for what he believed, and conventionality was not important. Butler notes with admiration the healthy appearance of the pioneers, their odd turns of phrase, the way they identify themselves with their sheep, and their basic shrewdness. He is attacked by the yen of the explorer: "As soon as I saw the mountains, I longed to get on the other side of them" (98), and he is proud of himself for roughing it so well. He describes the men living on the frontier as having a life that "appears a kind of mixture of that of a dog and that of an emperor, with a considerable predominance of the latter" (99). "There is much nonsense in the old country," he says, "from which people here are free. There is little conventionalism, little formality, and much liberality of sentiment; very little sectarianism . . ." (101).[40] Especially he enjoys his trips of exploration up several valleys looking for new sheep land.

Life in New Zealand

Once Butler had established his sheep run at "Mesopotamia," New Zealand, he spent much time at Christchurch.[41] He joined the Christchurch Club and came to know practically everyone of importance in the town. He rode with the top political dignitaries on the first trip of the railroad between Christchurch and Lyttleton. Considering the primitive conditions of his ranch, it is surprising that he took a piano there, dragging it on a bullock dray. Robert B. Booth in his *Five Years in New Zealand* says about a period he spent working for Butler: "Butler, Cook, and I would repair to the sitting-room [after supper] and round a glorious fire smoked or read or listened to Butler's piano. It was the most civilized experience I had had of up-country life."[42] L. J. Kennaway in *Crusts* describes Butler as "an explorer, who had seen some very hard times, and who, inside a sunburnt and wrinkled forehead, possessed far-thinking and acute brains."[43]

Butler himself was aware of the effect of his new experience. "A wider circle of ideas has resulted from travel," he writes to a friend, "and an entire uprooting of all past habits has been accompanied with a hardly less entire change of opinions upon many subjects. Firstly, I have lost all desire of making other people think the same as myself."[44] Again, he states: "I think I am a Unitarian now, but don't know and won't say; as for the Trinity I cannot make head or tail of it."[45] A year later he says: "For the present I renounce Christianity altogether. . . . I can only say that I have not found my digestion impeded since I have left off believing in what does not appear to be supported by sufficient evidence."[46]

Early Articles

In 1861 a newspaper called the *Press* was founded in Christchurch by James Edward FitzGerald, an intimate friend of Butler's. Like the *Eagle* at Cambridge, it became an outlet for occasional pieces by Butler who, Jones tells us,[47] was on one occasion in charge of it for some months during the editor's absence.

On 20 December 1862 the *Press* printed a dialogue by Butler entitled "Darwin on the Origin of Species." Purporting to be a discussion between two men who have read Darwin's book, one who liked it and one who did not, it is a clear, succinct statement of Darwin's chief arguments, combined with a cleverly dramatized but only slightly developed opposition to them. "C" (the critic) complains of Darwin's logicality, his monomania, his coldness, and his heartlessness, and concludes that he is "horrid" and "utterly subversive of Christianity." It is possible that "C" stands for "Cellarius," the pen name Butler had used in the *Eagle* and was to use again. "F" (the defender) points out that the struggle for survival is indeed ruthless, but he states that he believes in both Christianity and Darwin. Since the two appear to be irreconcilable, "the true course" must be "to use the freest candour in the acknowledgement of the difficulty; to estimate precisely its real value, and obtain a correct knowledge of its precise form. Then and then only is there a chance of any satisfactory result being obtained" (*A First Year,* 194).

Which of the two voices is Butler's? In a way, this is an unanswerable question: Since Butler created them both, he must have understood what each was saying; the issue is not resolved, only dramatized. Nevertheless, the impression was conveyed to many, including Darwin who somehow came into possession of a copy of the article, that it was a defense of, rather than an attack upon, the new theory of evolution. On 24 March 1863 Darwin sent a copy of the article to the editor of a magazine in England with the suggestion that—because it was "remarkable from its spirit and from giving so clear and accurate a view" of his theory—it deserved reprinting.[48]

According to Butler, three responses to his piece in the *Press* were probably written by Charles John Abraham, Bishop of Wellington (186). The first of these considers the Darwinian theory nothing "but a *réchauffée* of the old story that his namesake, Dr. [Erasmus] Darwin, served up in the end of the last century" (196); and it objects to the fact that Darwin's "fantasias . . . are made to come round at last to religious questions, with which really and truly they have nothing to do" (197). Butler, who replied in a letter signed "A.M.," criticized his own dialogue as rash, self-satisfied, and uninformed; and he then labeled the argument of his critic "disgraceful," pointing out that there is nothing about natural selection in the elder Darwin's work. Finally, he appealed to the reader to withhold judgment on the new theory

until the experts themselves had decided whether it was true or not
(198–201).

Butler's concealment of his authorship of the original dialogue when
writing again is typical. He liked best to work dramatically with ideas
to see how far they would go; already he was intrigued by the methods
of thought, by the drama of conflict. It is hard to believe that even
in 1863 he would have been willing to defer uncritically to the opinion
of experts, but he could certainly envision his argument as something
that would tell in a debate. Indeed, a trap lies open for any reader of
Butler who concludes from a single statement he may make that this
is his considered opinion, even at the time he makes it. Very often
Butler is merely testing his reader.

A letter signed "The Savoyard," which followed three weeks later,
gives a quotation from the elder Darwin's *Botanic Garden* that implies
a theory of natural selection (though teleological, not fortuitous, as
Charles's essentially was); and it may very well have been instrumental
in drawing Butler's attention to aspects of the earlier evolutionist's work
of which he was yet unaware. Four days later Butler replied. Evidently
he had not yet recognized the difference between the two natural
selections. But, as he was later to show, even Charles Darwin himself
did not successfully separate them. Butler points out to "The Savoyard"
that Dr. Erasmus Darwin's views are nothing but a speculation, whereas
Charles Darwin has gathered evidence for a well-organized theory that
can be appraised by the scientific world.

On 13 June Butler again contributed to the *Press*. This piece, entitled
"Darwin among the Machines," is signed "Cellarius." Perhaps in the
interim Butler has been meditating on the mechanical nature of the
Darwinian theory that allows only for chance variations; in any case,
this is the initial treatment of an idea exploited fully in *Erewhon*, namely,
that machines themselves can be seen undergoing an evolutionary process
from simple to complex. They get more and more efficient as the years
pass. And some even have rudimentary organs. The article suggests that
these machines may very well be man's successors: "we are daily giving
them greater power and supplying by all sorts of ingenious contrivances
that self-regulating, self-acting power which will be to them what
intellect has been to the human race. In the course of ages we shall
find ourselves the inferior race" (210). Thus man, Butler suggests, will
continue to exist, but only as the servant of the machine. Eventually,
he speculates, machines will develop so far that they will be able to
reproduce themselves. Already, he says, one machine is often employed

in making another. Since, therefore, it is perfectly evident that if machines are allowed to continue to develop they will dominate the world, he calls for war to the death against them. "Every machine of every sort should be destroyed. . . . Let there be no exceptions made, no quarter shown. . . . If it be urged that this is impossible under the present condition of human affairs, this at once proves that the mischief is already done, that our servitude has commenced in good earnest" (212–13). "Cellarius" concludes his piece with a deprecatory twist: "For the present, we shall leave this subject, which we present gratis to the members of the Philosophical Society. Should they consent to avail themselves of the vast field which we have pointed out, we shall endeavour to labour in it ourselves at some future and indefinite period" (213).

Joseph Jones speculates that a sarcastic review of *A First Year,* published in the *Press* for 28 April 1863, is by Butler too. "The vein of glib self-satisfied and thinly concealed conceit which runs through the whole volume," the reviewer says, "must render it almost amusingly nauseous even to the most charitable reader."[49] Butler, if he wrote this, was getting revenge for his father's careful editing and publication of the volume. Jones reprints also three other items from the *Press* of 1863 that he believes Butler wrote: "Darwin and the Novelists" (28 March), "From Our Mad Correspondent" (15 September), and a letter from "Nimmer Beschweift" (2 April), but his ascription is not persuasive.

Several months after his return to London Butler sent to the editors of the *Press* (29 July 1865) another article inspired by Darwinism called "Lucubratio Ebria." So tentative is his approach to the ideas proposed that he makes the suggestion that they may be nothing but a drunken dream. This allows him to spin out an amusing opening paragraph, but it may also reflect his own puzzlement over the intriguing thoughts that his mind had conceived. Again he hides his identity; again he attacks his own previous contribution, "Darwin among the Machines." But this time he defends an opposite point of view: He argues that machines, rather than being threats to the supremacy of mankind, are "the mode of development by which [the] human organism is most especially advancing, and every fresh invention is to be considered as an additional member of the resources of the human body" (*A First Year,* 217). This argument is based on the assumption that "The limbs of the lower animals have never been modified by any act of deliberation and forethought on their own part," but that, "when human intelligence stole like a late spring upon the mimicry of our semi-simious ancestry, the creature learnt how he could of his own forethought add extra-corporaneous limbs to the members of his own body" (215).

In a sense, Butler is probing the implications of a mechanically operated survival-of-the-fittest theory and is reducing it to absurdity. Why cannot machines be organisms, if organisms themselves have evolved by a mindless chance? Henceforth, Butler suggests, we might evaluate people on the relative complexity of their organization. A "really well-developed specimen of the race . . . will be furnished with a large box upon wheels, two horses, and a coachman" (218). In conclusion, though, he admits that there are other modes of judging men besides the organizational one. "Were we to go into this part of the question we should never have done," he says, "and we are compelled reluctantly to leave our dream in its present fragmentary condition" (220).

Butler restated the thesis of his "Darwin among the Machines" in "The Mechanical Creation," which appeared in the *Reasoner* (1 July 1865) in London. In it, as in "Lucubratio Ebria," he refers to his ideas as "half-shadow, half-substance," and says that he will leave "the intelligent reader to draw his own inferences" (231). He opens by suggesting that the form that future life may take is as difficult for men to imagine as animal life might have been for an observer who saw the world inhabited by nothing but plants. But, crossing the boundary that this suggests, he says that we may be living "in the first faint dawning" (232) of a new life which will be as different from men as they are from the vegetables. He argues that the rapid evolution of machines leading up to the steam engine which eats, breathes, and regulates itself is a clue to what is to come. "It cannot be said to be conscious, but the strides which it has made are made in the direction of consciousness" (233).

This article ends on a calmer note than did "Darwin among the Machines." Instead of calling for a revolt against machines before it is too late to stop their triumphant progress, Butler admits that, since personal advantage rightly dictates to each generation what it does, mankind must resign itself to a future in which it will be well treated by its machine masters who will require the services of men but will of necessity have evolutionary supremacy over them. At the end of the article he promises in a future piece "to regard machinery as a component part of the human organism" (237); he apparently meant to rework "Lucubratio Ebria" for his London audience.

The Return

In 1864 Butler became convinced that land and sheep values in New Zealand would fall and that if he waited much longer to sell out what he had acquired he might not make out well. Subsequent events proved him right. The £8,200 he now acquired from the sale of his holdings, invested at ten percent in the colony, would support him comfortably in London where he planned to pursue the art studies his father had refused to allow. On 15 June he left New Zealand, sailing on around the world via America on his way back to England.

Returning with him to England at his expense was Charles Paine Pauli, a subeditor of the *Press,* whom he had befriended. Butler continued to assist Pauli financially until Pauli's death in 1897, although for many years he could ill afford to do so. He had one of the major shocks of his life when he eventually discovered that Pauli had been sponging on him mercilessly during years when Pauli had actually been in no need whatever of financial assistance.[50] Sensing the possibility within himself for being exploited, which this friendship and the even more disastrous episode of his ill-advised financial speculations in Henry Hoare's companies proved an only too painful reality, Butler developed a stronger and stronger insistence upon the importance of worldly wisdom and shrewdness in money matters. These qualities, he felt, are part of the defense mechanism the man of imagination must erect to give him the freedom he needs in order to create.

On his arrival in London, Butler moved into the quarters at 15 Clifford's Inn which he was to occupy for the rest of his life. He immediately took up a simple routine of living that would allow him to do the work he wanted to do. His ambition at this time, and until 1877, was to prove that he had been right in desiring to become a painter. Attending art school and laboring many hours in the studio in his quarters, he worked diligently and long at this endeavor. The picture *Family Prayers* (*The Way of All Flesh,* Frontispiece), one of the first products of his renewed ambition, shows eight adults expressing varying degrees of boredom as they sit in the living room of his father's home listening to a paterfamilias (a clergyman) read from the Bible. Butler noted that if he had continued to paint out of his head, as he did in this picture, rather than to make academic studies from models, he "would have been all right."[51]

But he did not neglect his writing. A month after the last of his Darwinian articles had appeared, he grappled not with the evolution of organisms but with the evolution of opinions. In a piece called "Precaution in Free Thought" published by the *Reasoner* (1 August 1865), Butler considers the relativity of opinion (238–41). He takes the conservative position, one which seems to be becoming a necessity for him. He argues that although each generation must find out for itself its standard of right and should do what it can "to advance it in defiance of the world," care must be taken not to push for a growth that the roots will not support: "A sudden change of creed, unless a man is very clear indeed as to the steps by which he has changed it, is not unlikely to do him as much harm as good" (239). Referring specifically to the arguments for Christian miracles—which Jones states had concerned Butler in his university and New Zealand days[52]—he remarks that there must be a "screw loose" in every intellect that believes them.

Butler, nonetheless, points out that—since to deny these arguments is to bring a charge of stupidity, indolence, and cowardice against the age—one must proceed with great caution: "Loss of faith in the general right-mindedness and clear-headedness of one's age is a much more serious thing than loss of faith in a personal Deity" (240). Butler is thus telling himself, as well as his readers, to be cautious in the development of ideas, since solidarity is an essential hedge against insanity. A characteristic comment in this article is his observation that it is more dangerous to be opposed to the wealth of the country than to its thought: "It [wealth] is an august symbol. The universities, the public schools, the rampant Sabbatarianism of the age, the countless churches, the huge organizations of the various Christian creeds, are visible signs of one's own audacity" (239). Butler was becoming aware of what he himself would confront as his career developed.

That his doubts about religion were as important to him at this time as his playful explorations of the implications of Darwinism is shown by his printing at his own expense (his first venture into this kind of publication on his own) a pamphlet called "The Evidence for the Resurrection of Jesus Christ as Given by the Four Evangelists, Critically Examined," much of which he later incorporated into *The Fair Haven* (1873).[53] In the preface to this serious pamphlet he questions the sincerity of an age in which "no publisher of position will publish heresy so rank as mine,"[54] even though he is conscious of having done nothing more than to reason logically. Why cannot honest arguments be met by honest replies? He blames no one in particular: "No publisher of position can make them [Butler's arguments] public, even if he would, without doing himself a greater injury than he would be warranted in doing."[55]

As subsequent events were to show, Butler was not to give up the attempt to get a hearing for his ideas. Since direct statement went unheeded (his pamphlet failed completely), he would return to indirect statement, humor, and satire. He was also to seek to deepen his understanding of the reasons mankind could not tolerate a direct approach or a too rigid logic, so that he might learn to eschew these things himself. As Jones points out,[56] this pamphlet was Butler's apology for refusing to become a clergyman. At this point in his life he needed to get his reasons clearly stated. Darwin, who read the pamphlet, wrote Butler: "I particularly agree with all you say in your preface."[57]

Chapter Two
Erewhon

In 1870, at the advice of his doctor, Butler took an extended vacation on the Continent. In Venice he became acquainted with a Russian lady who on his departure said, "Et maintenant, Monsieur, vous allez créer." Butler's comment in his notes is: "Yes, but how to create? and what? I had not yet, for all my education, got to know that doing is the sole parent of doing, and creating a little the only way of learning how to create more; still, I went home resolved to do at any rate something in literature, if not in painting." Another push toward literature came from Sir Frederick Napier Broome, who, visiting England from New Zealand, called on Butler and in chatting with him suggested that he rewrite his *Press* articles.[1] Butler did this work on Sundays and holidays, while keeping up his painting as his main occupation. Early in 1871 he had nearly finished *Erewhon*.

Sometime before beginning this work he had formed a friendship with Miss Eliza Mary Ann Savage, whom he met at Heatherley's Art School. She had not liked him at first; but one day, when she met him on the street, he silently offered her some cherries from a basket out of which he was eating. She helped herself and went on her way rejoicing, also without a word; she now perceived that he was "different from anyone else."[2] Shortly they began to see more of each other, to exchange ideas, and to write letters which Butler carefully preserved. These letters provide an interesting record of his life up to 1885, the year of Miss Savage's death; and they were not only used by Jones in his biography but later published.[3]

Beginning with *Erewhon*, Miss Savage read the manuscript of each of Butler's books until her death in 1885, helping him with her intelligent comments and her unfailing enthusiasm for what he did.[4] The degree of her influence upon him will never be precisely known, but it is evident from the spriteliness of her many communications that she urged him in the direction of wit and satire—her own special bent, and also that she urged him to write fiction. Butler feared that she wished him to marry her, which he was not prepared to do; she, on the other hand, seems to have been happy enough with the friendship he offered and to have desired nothing more.[5] Still, the two sonnets that Butler wrote about her in 1901 while going over the letters they had sent to each other suggest a lack of warmth on his part hard to forgive, in spite of Festing Jones's protest that he was "the dearest, kindest, most considerate friend . . . never selfish or egotistic."[6]

Butler sent the manuscript of *Erewhon* to the publishing house of Chapman and Hall which, on the advice of its reader, George Meredith, rejected it. Butler's characteristic comment about this rejection was that it was not strange; he would have rejected Meredith's work if it had been submitted to him. Although Trübner published *Erewhon* in 1872, it was not at the firm's own risk.[7] However, it was a success, not only because the unsigned first edition was thought to be by Lord Lytton,[8] but also because of its merits. It was the only book by Butler that brought him a profit, and nine editions were printed during his lifetime, eight with minor revisions, but the ninth (1901) with considerable rewriting and many additions.

The complexity of *Erewhon*—part ordinary satire, part utopian romance, and part satire of utopias—has confused readers. But the book hangs together: it is an account in imaginative form of the freeing experience that Butler's rebellion against his family, his trip to New Zealand, and his reading of Darwin were for him. It also expresses his desire as an artist to share that experience with his readers. Also, as Ruth Gounelas states, "The theme of the absurdity of extreme positions is of fundamental significance . . . it gives the work a unity and consistency with which it is rarely credited."[9]

Transformation

The opening chapters of *Erewhon,* which is far more than a mere reworking of Butler's previous articles, present tellingly the psychology of transformation in symbolic terms—the transition from a world where things are in their places to the new realm of Erewhon where the ground rules are changed. Before the trip starts, in a woodshed, said to be like a cathedral, and with one votive candle burning in it—thus suggesting a religious transformation—the narrator gets his first inkling of what may lie ahead for him as he watches Chowbok, the Maori guide, sitting statuelike on the bales of wool and grimacing frightfully. Once the trip has started, there are two treacherous valleys to cross— spiritual dangers—and the narrator must lose his guide and go on alone before he can assail the second valley. It is by mere chance that he goes onward, a magic chance, for the clouds open only momentarily to reveal "a glimpse of an immeasurable extent of blue and distant plains" (20). "Had I arrived five minutes later, the cloud would have been over the pass, and I should not have known of its existence."

As he goes down the cliff, the narrator becomes so horrified by the strangeness of his surroundings that he momentarily loses his head. Later, when he camps in the ravine, he realizes that he cannot return. "It is a dreadful feeling that of being cut off from all one's kind. . . . I do not believe that any man could long retain his reason in such solitude. . . . One begins doubting one's own identity" (23). During the night he dreams of a gigantic organ thundering "arpeggioed harmonics" on the mountainside, and a voice says "It is Handel"—the man who really guides Butler through his life and his work.

When the narrator awakes, he hears the ghostly sound the wind makes blowing through the ten statues at the pass into Erewhon—the Ten Commandments of the Old Testament, we surmise, which by formalizing our lives, Butler suggests, have kept us from coming nearer to ourselves. We must pass these and leave them behind; we ought not to be frightened by them since they are really only hollow bogeymen. "I had a far worse time of it than I have told [the reader] and I strongly recommend him to remain in Europe if he can" (25); that is, remain in the realm of accepted thoughts. Crossing the turbulent river, the narrator again loses control and is almost drowned; he tells us that he cannot "remember anything at all save flying over furious waters." When he reaches the opposite bank, he says, "How I got there I do not know" (1872 ed.).[10] Finally he ascends to the pass into Erewhon and sees the ten stone statues. "I believe I fainted," he says, "for how long I shall never know. I was deadly sick and cold when I came to myself. . . . I am afraid I cried out. I felt sure that I could never get back alive" (1872 ed.).

These details deserve notice: they are a symbolic treatment of Butler's dangerous and frightening movement out of the convictions of his youth and his era and out of the pre-Darwinian world. The emotional overtones are all too clear. The journey is a traumatic one into the reversals of unconscious perception. Later the narrator is able to laugh at the trick the statues played on him (38). Once across the pass, man can come, at least in part, to himself. Do not forget that the subtitle of *Erewhon* is *Over the Range*.

A New World

The people of Erewhon are happy, healthy, and beautiful. Their beauty suggests that they are right to treat all illness with the cruelty with which Europeans treat crime. The judge in an Erewhonian court who condemns a man suffering from tuberculosis to life imprisonment with hard labor and two tablespoons of castor oil daily and refuses to listen to how he became ill—the only question is, is he ill or not?—is in one way a satirical portrait of judges who condemn robbers and terrorists in our world while refusing to consider what social inequities made them thus or whether a jail term will cure them. But the Erewhonians prosper under their "infinitely absurd" conditions (83–87), whereas we do not. Alternately, the trial may also be a comment on the moral blindness of "survival of the fittest." *Erewhon* indeed, as already observed, hovers between satire and utopia, and the narrator's frequent inability to get the point of what he reports and observes, as when he calls the Erewhonians "absurd," simply adds another dimension to its equivocations. That Butler, the author, was himself serious is suggested in a 1900 comment: "I . . . was surprised (and I may add, shocked) that anyone could doubt my having been serious—very much so—in my own way."[11]

Of course it is this "in my own way" that has baffled readers. To illustrate the complex ways in which *Erewhon* mixes satire and utopia, take its treatment of crime, providing "straighteners" who through a regimen of confessions, discussions, and chastisement can cure wealthy bankers who embezzle from widows, much as we provide medical men for illness. This is a strikingly original proposal suggesting valuable reform. *Erewhon*, again, seems to suggest that we too would be better off if our lip service to religion were replaced by the Erewhonian devotion to Mrs. Grundy rather than to the "absurdities" of their musical banks. The clergyman in the musical bank who is infuriated at a tip given in musical currency but delighted at a gift of "real" money can be a clue to the extent of our own hypocrisy. The point should be made here that the version of *Erewhon* in widest circulation is the 1901 revision into which Butler put passages championing his biological theories, giving the book even more complexity than it had in 1872, and adding another "way" to the multiple responses we must be prepared to make to it.

Butler's imagination in *Erewhon* throws much light on reality, as does the imagination of Lewis Carroll in *Alice in Wonderland* (1865), but

Butler's world is "over the range," rather than "down a rabbit hole" or "through a looking glass." It anticipates and exercises the same kind of power as did the findings of later anthropologists and sociologists about the relativity of ethical codes and human behavior, findings which can frighten people and anger them. Danger lurks. After his second visit to Erewhon in *Erewhon Revisited,* the narrator, then called Higgs, suffers a complete mental collapse, as does also John Pickard Owen in *The Fair Haven.*

The Erewhonians insist upon personifying everything they regard as admirable or anything they do not understand. Our hero reasons with Arowhena by arguing that personification does not explain the operation of the ideal nor of that which is not understood. Later, when he has explained his own religion to her, she turns his argument back upon him, criticizing his conception of God. She says "that people would no more cease to love God on ceasing to believe in His objective personality, than they had ceased to love justice on discovering that she was not really personal; nay, that they would never truly love Him till they saw Him thus" (127). In the 1901 edition Butler added the following passage, which expresses his final faith as well as anything else he wrote:

Nevertheless, her remarks have haunted me, and I have since met with many very godly people who have had a great knowledge of divinity, but no sense of the divine: and again, I have seen a radiance upon the face of those who were worshipping the divine either in art or nature—in picture or statue—in field or cloud or sea—in man, woman, or child—which I have never seen kindled by any talking about the nature and attributes of God. Mention but the word divinity, and our sense of the divine is clouded. (128)

In another chapter Butler enlarges his discussion of Ydgrun (Mrs. Grundy). In it, his desire to judge men for what they are, not what they pretend to be, emerges most strongly. He is actually praising the well-rounded Englishman of his day:

They [the Ydgrunites] were gentlemen in the full sense of the word; and what has one not said in saying this? . . . Being strong, and handsome, and kindly nurtured, moreover being inured from youth to exercises and athletics of all sorts, and living fearlessly under the eye of their peers, among whom there exists a high standard of courage, generosity, honour, and every good and manly quality—what wonder that they should have become, so to speak, a law unto themselves; and, while taking an elevated view of the goddess Ydgrun, they should have gradually lost all faith in the recognized deities of their country? . . . The example of a real gentleman is, if I may say so without profanity, the best of all gospels. (130–32, with addition from 1872 ed.)

Yet the narrator desires to convert even these ideal men and to save them from "their certain perdition."

The Erewhonians regard the doctrine of immortality as immoral because it would lead people to think this life of secondary importance. But, just as Christians believe in an afterlife, they have a mythology of preexistence, and profess to believe that it is the pestering of the unborn that causes parents to have children. The birth formula to which all children must subscribe exonerates their parents from any blame in their birth. The child vows that "he did with malice aforethought set himself to plague and pester two unfortunate people who had never wronged him, and who were quite contented and happy until he conceived this base design against their peace; for which wrong he now humbly entreats their pardon" (137). This mythology of the unborn describes the suffering both to parents and to the children caused by mismatches decreed by fate, just as Butler himself suffered from a mismatched father; it also warns the would-be infant of the certainty of death, of the burden of free will, and of the miseries of life that those who desire to leave the realm of the unborn will bring upon themselves. The only consolation for one who has unwisely chosen to be born is that, if he will do his "present and immediate duty" each day of his life, he may safely get through the trials that lie ahead of him. All of this suggests Butler's meditations on the tragedies of Victorian family life as he had experienced them.

The Erewhonians, like their European mirror images, have an absurd educational system in their "Colleges of Unreason," one aim of which is to incapacitate young people so that they will be unable to lead useful lives, just as English education insisted on large doses of Latin and Greek with no attention to the practical arts. But the Erewhonians are far more conscious of what they are doing than Europeans are. Mr. Thims, who takes the narrator through the university, explains that the students are drilled in "hypothetics," which enlarges their horizons by presenting them with "a set of utterly strange and impossible contingencies" (162). The students are taught a synthetic language of no conceivable use, and they are drilled in the principles of "unreason" on the premise that "there is hardly an error into which men may not

easily be led if they base their conduct upon reason only" (164).
Although the buildings at the university are so beautiful as to have "a
hallowing and refining influence which is in itself half an education"
(170), the professors "seemed to devote themselves to the avoidance
of every opinion with which they were not perfectly familiar, and
regarded their brains as a sort of sanctuary, to which if an opinion had
once resorted, none other was to attack it" (170).

Machines or Organisms?

At the university the narrator discusses the revolt against the machines
with a learned professor of antiquities. He is given "The Book of the
Machines" which presents the entire story. This part of *Erewhon* reminds
the reader of Carlyle's *Sartor Resartus:* There is an elaborate mystification
about omitted passages, editorial changes, apologies, and explanations,
as though Butler, like Carlyle, had to stand at a distance from his
material to insure his control of it. The reasoning presented to show
that machines may indeed be the next stage in evolutionary development
is more compelling and detailed than in Butler's early articles on this
subject. After citing numerous analogies between the behavior of living
organisms and the behavior of machines, the Erewhonian writer asks
"Whether strictly speaking we should not ask what kind of levers a
man is made of rather than what is his temperament?" (179). Then,
Butler has the narrator tell us, the author "became more and more
obscure, so that I was obliged to give up all attempt at translation"
(179).

The narrator again essays translation, and he gives a passage in which
the Erewhonian savant points out that such organs as the eye and the
brain serve the individual much as machines do—they are comparable
to microscopes, telescopes, or mechanical computers. Then suddenly he
views the body as a whole congeries of machines: "Our blood is
composed of infinite living agents which go up and down the highways
and byways of our bodies as people in the streets of a city." (183).
Once more our hero interposes: "Here the writer became again so
hopelessly obscure that I was obliged to miss several pages" (183).
Again we face the paradox of Darwinism: Are organisms, which evolve
by mere chance, purely mechanical, or are machines themselves organic
and alive?

"The Book of the Machines" resumes by warning that, although it
is now impossible to do away with all machines, their development

must be stopped if they are to be prevented from winning mastery over mankind: "How many men at this hour are living in a state of bondage to the machines?" (185). "Consider . . . the colliers and pitmen and coal merchants and coal trains, and the men who drive them, and the ships that carry coals—what an army of servants do the machines thus employ! Are there not probably more men engaged in tending machinery than in tending men?" (186). The Erewhonian savant discusses the objection to his line of reasoning that says that machines are not organic because they cannot reproduce themselves, and he counters by asking how many "machines are there which have not been produced systematically by other machines?" (188). If it is replied that man makes them do so, the answer is that there are "whole families of plants [which would] die out if their fertilization were not effected by a class of agents utterly foreign to themselves" (188). The argument that a thimble cannot make another thimble is met by pointing out that "very few creatures reproduce after their own kind." Thus "the butterfly lays an egg, which egg can become a caterpillar, which caterpillar can become a chrysalis, which chrysalis can become a butterfly" (189).

A little later in the argument the narrator again finds "a very long and untranslatable digression" (192) about the different races and families of machines. This is followed by a discussion of free will that culminates in the conclusion that man is really no freer than the machine. Finally the point is made that we have come to depend on machines ourselves so that "it is the machines which act upon man and make him man, as much as man who has acted upon and made the machines" (199). To prevent a dishonorable future of slavery, we must destroy these machines now, no matter at what cost to ourselves; we must not give in to those who argue that slavery is better than death. Thus revolution is decreed.

"The Book of the Machines" is the most brilliant part of *Erewhon,* a virtuosic replaying of Butler's New Zealand meditations and writings on Darwinism as well as a remarkable foreshadowing of his later books. Here the "untranslatable" sections suggest the as yet untranslatable confusion in Butler's own mind and in ours too when we meditate upon the transformation science has caused by saying that human beings, in all their pride, are merely levers and the result of blind chance; alternately that computers, the ultimate machines, may acquire intelligence and become as organic as any organism. What indeed would the Erewhonian savant think of nuclear weapons, the ultimate of all machines?

At this point in his presentation the narrator builds a balloon and escapes from Erewhon, hearing in the mist over the ocean "the last few bars of the first part of the minuet in *Saul*' (1872 ed.).[12] Thus his guardian angel, Handel, whose organ playing he had heard as he entered the country, is with him as he leaves.

Interpretations

We now have before us the working out of a whole set of satirical and utopian notions. We may surmise that Butler made his book as complex and fantastic as it is because he did not dare to face up to the total implications of his ideas. Certainly if the Erewhonian mood should become too extreme in anyone, allowing him to question every human relation and to stand everything on its head, alienation might result (some have in fact concluded that Butler himself was more than a little out of his mind). Here no doubt lies the reason for our author's approval of the "High Ydgrunites."

Hans-Peter Breuer[13] and Herbert Sussman[14] argue that Butler did not realize until after *Erewhon* was published that viewing machines as having their own evolutionary development, as he does in "The Book of the Machines," implied that Darwin was omitting from his consideration the elements of consciousness, foresight, and volition that had previously defined organic life. Butler's own statement in the preface to the second edition denying that he had meant to criticize Darwin supports this view. Breuer goes so far as to see *Erewhon* as primarily an extended spoof of the whole method of arguing from analogy so brilliantly used by William Paley and Joseph Butler,[15] whose books Butler had studied in his theology courses, books not without influence also on Darwin's method of reasoning. Sussman argues that in *Erewhon* Butler sought "only to play upon the paradoxes of philosophical mechanism rather than resolve them."[16] One is forced, however, to agree with G. N. Sharma[17] that "The 'Book of the Machines' . . . is central to the artistic and moral economy of *Erewhon,* to the projection of Butler's satiric as well as his utopian vision."[18] The Erewhonians are so happy, so healthy, so attractive, so close to the Victorian ideal of a "pastoral Utopia," not only because of their wonderful ability to compromise, but also because they banned all recent machines, though retaining the useful earlier ones: no world of smog, unemployment, atomic bombs for them!

But from the start *Erewhon* was criticized not in terms of what it is but in terms of what critics thought it should be. The *Academy* for 1 August 1872 found the novel's narrative lacking in sustained power; its satire inconsistent, since not all the features of European society are shown in reverse; and its attempt to portray an ideal society a failure because the Erewhonians are not ideal—if they were, they would not punish their sick. The reviewer called *Erewhon* "a dull book throughout." The *Athenaeum*[19] also called it "slovenly" because of its inconsistencies, complained of its attack on Darwinism, and recommended that its author return to sheep farming and give up writing altogether. The *British Quarterly Review*[20] expressed bewilderment: "The effect of the whole is disappointing, where it is not unintelligible . . . we are utterly at a loss to see the relevance or meaning of many of the illustrations selected. Either they are simply unmeaning or absolutely foolish." The *Fortnightly Review*[21] called the book the work of a beginner that could easily have been made better if the author had taken pains with it. It has "plenty of good points in detail, but no particular point on the whole." The *Saturday Review,*[22] which objected to the immorality of the treatment of vice and virtue, called *Erewhon* too farfetched and complicated. The *Spectator*[23] praised it as the ablest book of its sort since Swift, but called its author a "universal sceptic" who was opposed to all abstract thought, all religion, all principles of morality. Those who take its teaching seriously, the reviewer said, will find themselves in Erewhon—nowhere—when they have done.

These samples of the critical remarks, which constitute the best "press" Butler received during his lifetime, indicate clearly what he confronted in writing such challenging books as *The Fair Haven* and *The Way of All Flesh*—and how careful he would have to be if he aspired to favorable attention. As he came to realize, originality is always puzzling to the guardians of the status quo. This realization caused Butler in his 1901 revision of *Erewhon* to include some comments on originality: "genius was like offences—needs must that it come, but woe unto that man through whom it comes. A man's business, they hold, is to think as his neighbors do" (165). Butler slowly discovered that, if he were to have an audience at all, it would be a future audience. At the same time he continued to do everything he could, short of compromising himself, to win readers; and the amount of review space that was given to his books is actually somewhat surprising. A lone wolf, paying his way with his publishers, would not fare so well in the 1980s as Butler did over a century ago.

Butler feared that his "Book of the Machines" would distress Charles Darwin. Two months after *Erewhon* appeared, he wrote Darwin to say that he had developed these ideas "for mere fun . . . without a particle of serious meaning" and that he had aimed his satire at Bishop Butler's *Analogy of Religion* but had not dared to make this clear in his book.[24] In the preface to the second edition (June 1872) he said that "nothing could be further from my intention . . . than any attempt to laugh at Mr. Darwin" (xix). The subsequent direction of Butler's work certainly raises a question as to whether, when he made these comments, he really understood his own intention. Was he simply being diplomatic, or was he being true only to a superficial awareness of himself? He later said that no author in the flush of a first success is to be trusted with the writing of a preface. But the immediate result was that Darwin invited him to his home for a weekend, the first of the two visits Butler paid him.

Chapter Three
Major Challenges

As time went on, Butler learned the importance of doing what an inner urge asked him to do, of starting whatever that urge asked him to start, and then seeing what developed. The idea of doing this appears to have been an empirical discovery made by self-observation, rather than a reflection of the romantic notion of inspiration. Throughout his life Butler had little use for romantic notions: in temperament he belonged to the solid generations of the eighteenth century.[1] But he learned to listen to his deeper intimations; the ability to do this became one of his major discoveries and led to his *Life and Habit* theory of unconscious memory. Those who deny the existence for Butler of this subliminal urge, who call it merely paradoxical or a "hobby-horse idea,"[2] miss a great deal that is important in him.

The Fair Haven

Butler wrote to Miss Savage that the idea for *The Fair Haven* was an idea "which I must work out or die."[3] We surmise that the failure of his pamphlet "The Evidence for the Resurrection of Jesus Christ as Contained in the Four Evangelists Critically Examined" to attract any attention compelled him to a continuing effort to justify his refusal to enter the ministry. His attempt was to build on the success of *Erewhon* and to prepare an ironical or satirical presentation of the pamphlet material in the hope that thus he would win an audience, even though at this time writing was only a weekend hobby, his main endeavor still being to become a painter. For the time being he dropped his Darwinian speculations.

What he now did was to create an elaborate hoax: he imposed two imaginary authors, John Pickard Owen and William Bickersteth Owen, between himself and the material of his pamphlet, and to complicate matters further he pretended that the detailed analysis of the evidences for the resurrection was designed not to destroy faith in the miraculous but to strengthen it. Then he added a dissertation on the Christ Ideal done in a parody of sentimental religious writing designed to be a fitting satirical climax. All of these are clever tricks to play, and there is abundant evidence from the notes and letters to prove that Butler played them on purpose,[4] but the tricks are too complex and there is little doubt that they got out of control.[5]

A deeper reason for the lack of control than the failure in literary skill lies in the fact that, in spite of his bravado, Butler remained all his life genuinely ambiguous about religion. The ambiguity flaws what might have been a major work, even though the preface to the second edition lays the cards on the table and holds up to ridicule those reviewers who took the book to be a serious defense of Christianity. In this preface Butler pretends to be shocked that anyone could think it a satire: "This is very dreadful, but what can one do?" (xxi).

The "Memoir of the Late John Pickard Owen," which opens *The Fair Haven,* is the most effective section of the volume. Really a novel in miniature, it presents several living characters. We are made aware early in the "Memoir" of the genuine shock to John, a sincere and clear-thinking youngster, when he discovers that life is not what it pretends to be: that women are not "all solid woman" (6) but have legs beneath their elaborate skirts and petticoats; that chicken and sheep are not solid meat as they should be but are "mere skin and bone covering a cavern" (7); and that grown-ups are not above saying their prayers when children are watching but not saying them when they think they are unobserved (10). What a shock to discover that the world is a bundle of pretenses! Further, what a shock to discover that one's conception of God is modeled on one's conception of one's father (8), and that Evangelical literalism is "the main obstacle to the complete overthrow of unbelief"! (3).

Mrs. Owen's daydreams of her sons as Christian martyrs and of herself as the elect of God reveal a genuinely disagreeable character, although John's brother, William Bickersteth Owen, never tires of protesting his devotion to her. Her literal faith in the Bible and her respect for honesty and book learning set her son John an impossible goal that forces him, because of the unrelenting rigor of his mind, "to give up not only his mother but Christ Himself for Christ's sake" (15). After John discovers that baptism has no discernible effect on the characters of those baptized and passes through various religious phases, William comments that John's mental anguish resulted directly from his never having been taught to see more than one side of a question— as the youthful Butler had never been taught. When, years later, John wins through beyond his deism to genuine broad-mindedness, he looks upon young people who already have mental freedom and remarks: "With a great sum obtained I this freedom; but thou wast free-born" (19). Yet, adds William, John gained something from his suffering: "Awakening to the perception of the whole after an intimate acquaintance with the details, he was able to realize the position and meaning of all that he had hitherto experienced in a way which has been vouchsafed to few, if any others. . . . He was as one who has made the circuit of a mountain, and yet been ascending during the whole time of his doing so: such a person finds himself upon the same side as at first, but upon a greatly higher level" (20–21).

John Pickard Owen's great discovery, which emerges from the mental anguish he endures, is that the discrepancies and inconsistencies he finds in the Bible strengthen rather than weaken faith, "inasmuch as the true spiritual conception in the mind of man could be indirectly more certainly engendered by a strife, a warring, a clashing, so to speak, of versions, all of them distorting slightly some one or other of the features of the original, than directly by the most absolutely correct impression which human language could convey" (22). Again, satire apart, this is close to the pragmatic view of truth Butler himself was later to defend so strongly.

Yet Butler is indeed making fun of John Pickard Owen for his willingness to find strength in inconsistencies, and thus also of himself. The skill with which John traces the inconsistencies in the Gospels— for this is his central topic—is only equaled by the sanctimonious glibness with which John justifies the inconsistencies by attributing them to divine will and wisdom. Butler imitates to perfection the high-flown, self-satisfied rhetoric of the higher criticism; and the whole argument becomes a travesty of right reason, since it assumes the very thing the miracles are supposed to prove—namely, the truth of the Christian story. Armed with his preposterous theory, John finds that the arguments that lead so many to atheism become for him the "foundation-stone of faith." He is a veritable Don Quixote of religion, persuaded that a magician has turned Dulcinia into a milkmaid, or like Philip H. Gosse who convinced himself that fossil remains had been planted in the earth to test man's faith.[6] Surely contradictions among the Gospel accounts cannot in themselves prove the wisdom of God, and we must laugh at anyone foolish enough to think so.

Actually, *The Fair Haven* is a virtuoso attack on human reason, using the theological arguments so dear to the Victorians but calculated to make the head of any careful reader spin. Filled with analogies drawn from painting and music and science, it probes again and again at the basis of the rational process and comes close to suggesting that the mind cannot arrive at any truth at all. It is a highly artistic, controlled presentation of the mental anguish that had tormented the author himself for fourteen years; it is also an early example of the sort of exploration of the logical processes that was to be carried further by later psychological and philosophical writers. William James would have enjoyed it and might even have been led to question his own "Will to Believe."[7]

William Bickersteth Owen tells us that John was delighted to find that Dean Alford not only admitted an irreconcilable conflict between the Gospels of St. Luke and St. Matthew but also said that he believed them both (26). John contends that Dean Alford, without being fully aware of it, was right in realizing that "the spiritual value of each account was no less precious for not being in strict accordance with the other," and that what counts is "the subjective truth conveyed by both the narratives, which lives in our hearts independently of precise knowledge concerning the actual facts" (27). Surely there is some truth in this view.

What is reality? This is a question that the nineteenth century kept asking. Its probing culminated in F. H. Bradley's *Appearance and Reality,* the final statement of absolute idealism, in which all contradictions merge. Butler, in a nonacademic fashion, was on a similar path. Thus John Pickard Owen was "alternately under the influence of two conflicting spirits—at one time writing as though there were nothing precious under the sun except logic . . . at another leading the reader almost to believe that he disregarded the value of any objective truth. . . . Whenever he was in one mood he seemed to forget the possibility of any other" (29). From one point of view, this presentation of the conflict between logic and faith is Butler's evaluation in 1873 of the state of mind that eight years earlier had led him to write his Resurrection pamphlet; from another, it is his attempt to put the material of this pamphlet into a satiric setting.

One section of the "Memoir" presents a group of quotations from John's commonplace book, written before he regained his faith. Many of John's thoughts about Christianity and about Roman and Greek ideals appear in the notes Butler began to collect a few years after the appearance of *The Fair Haven.* For example, in March 1883, Butler wrote: "The Song of Solomon and the book of Esther are the most interesting in the Old Testament, but these are the very ones that make the smallest pretensions to holiness, and even these are neither of them of very transcendent merit. . . . Ecclesiastes contains some fine things but is strongly tinged with pessimism, cynicism, and affectation . . . the Psalms generally are poor and, for the most part, querulous, spiteful, and introspective into the bargain" (*Note-Books,* 201). John Pickard Owen likewise complains, "The parables which every one praises are in reality very bad: The Unjust Steward, the Labourers in the Vineyard, the Prodigal Son, Dives and Lazarus, the Sower and the Seed . . . are all either grossly immoral, or tend to engender a very low estimate of the character of God" (*The Fair Haven,* 39). And he adds, "The value of generosity and magnanimity was perfectly well known among the ancients, nor do these qualities assume any nobler guise in the teaching of Christ than they did in that of the ancient heathen philosophers" (39). He then states that the Christian emphasis on self-denial is a poor substitute for "generosity and high spirit" (40), and he questions whether Christianity has done anything at all to contribute to the spread of these qualities: "The ideal presented by the character of Christ . . . offers but a peevish view of life and things in comparison with that offered by other highest ideals—the old Roman and Greek ideals, the Italian ideal, and the Shakespearean ideal" (41).

Butler hoped, of course, that planting questions about the merits of the Christian ideal in a book ostensibly defending the miraculous element in Christianity would cause readers to reevaluate their convictions. John finally attempts to redefine Christianity: "It is only conventional Christianity which will stand a man in good stead to live by; true Christianity will never do so. . . . And what if some unhappy wretch, with a serious turn of mind and no sense of the ridiculous, takes all this talk about Christianity in sober earnest, and tries to act on it? Into what misery may he not easily fall, and with what life-long errors may he not embitter the lives of his children!" (44–45). On all this, his brother William, but not Samuel Butler, comments: "His mind was indeed in darkness!" (46).

After this introductory material comes John Pickard Owen's account of the growth of infidelity in his day. He tells us that the reasoning of Bishop Butler and of Paley—those eighteenth-century authors who had attempted reasoned defences of Christianity against the strictures of the Deists and the scientists of their day—is no longer convincing in his era, and he explains that only he who fully understands the position of the faithless man will be able to win him back to faith—his arguments must be comprehended before they can be refuted.

The irony, of course, is that Butler means the opposite of what John says: Once we fully understand the position of the faithless man we ourselves will hardly be won back to faith. John embarks on a long and detailed statement of the reasons the faithless man has for rejecting the miracle of the Resurrection, remarking at frequent intervals that he is reserving his answering argument, calculated to demolish his position, until the end. First he elaborately refutes the "hallucination theory" of Strauss, arguing that since the ardent faith of the Apostles arose as a result of the Resurrection, it cannot be reckoned a cause of the Apostles' thinking that they saw Christ alive when they really did not. David Strauss, a German theologian, had actually attempted in his 1835 *Leben Jesu (Life of Jesus)* to prove the Gospel story to be mythological, not real.

Having silenced Strauss, our amateur theologian next takes up the issue of the discrepancies among the various Gospel accounts of the Resurrection. Again the argument is acute and vigorous. He draws on "an anonymous pamphlet" of 1865 (Butler's own) and subjects the Gospel accounts, Dean Alford's notes, and the German commentators to minute scrutiny just as Butler had done. His constant plea is that we face up to the facts, and his chief delight is to point out that no one so far has done so. The acuteness of his reasoning about such a matter as the wound in the Saviour's side and Dean Alford's "disgraceful" notes on it reminds us of the perverted ingenuity of Dostoyevski's Smerdyakov in *The Brothers Karamazov*. There is no good reply to be made to this probing analysis, any more than there is to Smerdyakov's, but we are amazed at the mind of one who can indulge in it.

John likens Dean Alford to "a disreputable attorney," but then he shifts the blame onto theologians in general: "One would have thought he [Dean Alford] could have been guilty of nothing short of infatuation in hoping that the above notes would pass muster with any ordinarily intelligent person . . . [but] his confidence has not been misplaced. Of all those engaged in the training of our young men for Holy Orders . . . whose very profession it is to be lovers of truth and candour . . . *not a single one,* so far as I know, has raised his voice in protest. If a man has not lost his power of weeping, let him weep for this" (153–54). "No truthful mind can doubt," he concludes, "that the cause of Christ is far better served by exposing an insufficient argument than by silently passing it over" (154).

Here John is chastising Dean Alford and all theologians for their disregard for fact; but then in the conclusion of the work for which he has kept us waiting so long he praises the Bible for precisely this disregard. Thus the strangest quality of *The Fair Haven,* if viewed as the satire which in many of its details it assuredly is, is that Butler himself through the rest of his life never ceased to explore the possibility of seeing truth in the terms he has set forth here—not in logical isolation as a thing in itself, but as a give-and-take of forces and as something that relates to the accumulated wisdom of mankind. So, in spite of the sanctimonious tone of John's argument at the end and in spite of the fact that he never meets the unfaithful on his own grounds— as he had all along promised to do—he speaks in Butler's voice. It is satire, but what a many-voiced satire it is: satire of the literalist method of attacking Strauss and Dean Alford, satire of John's overblown pietism, and satire of Butler's own growing way of defining the truth. *The Fair Haven* explores an internal debate with the issues unresolved.

The presence of some of Butler's most characteristic attitudes toward truth and reality does not prevent John Pickard Owen from relapsing into "a religious melancholy which nothing could disturb" and dying "in a state little better than idiocy" (56). To heighten the satire of his own Butlerianism, Butler includes in *The Fair Haven* a chapter on "The Christ-Ideal" so platitudinous that he himself characterized it as "the kind of rubbish that would go down with the *Spectator.*"[8]

Butler hoped that his book would be attacked. He then would have, he said, "an opportunity for excusing myself; and, if so, I shall endeavour that the excuse may be worse than the fault it is intended to excuse."[9] But no attack of this sort was forthcoming, though the *Academy* condemned the book as an immoral performance, just as it had condemned *Erewhon.*[10] The *Rock* and the *Scotsman* reviewed it as a serious defense of Christianity; the reviewer in the *National Reformer* was puzzled by it; and the author of a pamphlet entitled *Jesus versus Christianity* recognized its satiric purpose (xix–xxi). Charles Darwin, to whom Butler sent a copy, wrote Butler: "It has interested me greatly and is extremely curious. If I had not known that you had written it I should not even have suspected that the author was not orthodox, within the wide stated limits. . . . What has struck me much in your book is your dramatic power . . . the way in which you earnestly and thoroughly assume the character and think the thoughts of the man you pretend to be."[11]

These responses, especially Darwin's, underline the book's failure as a satire since real satire, while appearing to say one thing, must be clearly understood to say the opposite. But if *The Fair Haven* is taken not just as satire but as presenting a dramatic struggle with the paradoxes of religious faith and the paradoxes of truth itself, then it has much meaning. The reviewers missed this meaning. In actuality, *The Fair Haven's* subtlety qualifies it as one of Butler's most characteristic books.

Financial Crisis

Butler continued to paint at Heatherley's Art School, and his picture *Mr. Heatherley's Holiday* was exhibited at the Royal Academy in 1874, along with the portrait, *A Child's Head;* but in order to write he gave up the hour in the evening during which he had been wont to play the piano. Late in 1873, however, he began having financial troubles that took his attention from his writing. Wishing to keep a closer watch over the investment of his capital with the hope of increasing his income, he recalled from New Zealand the £8,330 to which his capital had now grown and later invested it in a number of companies recommended to him by a banker-friend, Henry Hoare.[12] These investments soon proved the greatest financial error of his life. Instead of prospering, the companies failed; and in the spring of 1874 Henry Hoare failed with them. There was, however, a possibility of retrieving some of the loss if the Canada Tanning Extract Company, of which Butler had been made a director, could be put on its feet. In June he sailed for Canada to see what could be done. In July he returned briefly to London to report to the board of directors. He was given full power to act, and by 5 August, in Montreal once more, he was writing to Miss Savage: "I have fallen among thieves. Well, I believe I may also truly say that the thieves have fallen among *me.*"[13]

In May 1875 he again returned to London for a board meeting, and in December he left Montreal for good. Although he had reduced the company's expenses by £1,600 a year, it could not be saved, and, when final settlement was made, he had remaining to him only £2,000 of his fortune.[14] Now he could no longer live on his income as he had previously done; he had to dip into his capital, which thus gradually diminished.

By 1879 Butler's troubles were so serious that he had to appeal to his father for help. When he was still an undergraduate at Cambridge, his family had persuaded him to sign an agreement permitting the sale of the Whitehall mansion and six acres of land. This was a valuable part of an estate left by Butler's grandfather to come to the author by revision on the deaths of his father and aunt who, in the meantime, enjoyed the income from the property but could not sell it without Butler's consent. Butler now felt that he was entitled to something from his father as indemnity for a step he had been persuaded to take when he was too young to know his own rights in the matter. After much discussion, Canon Butler agreed to allow him £300 a year. In 1881, however, the property in question was resettled to give him an absolute revision on which he could borrow, and once this was done his father did not need to give him anything more. Finally, in 1886, when his father died, he inherited the property left him by his grandfather and his financial worries were at an end.

Four Books on Evolution

Immediately after *The Fair Haven* was published, Butler had begun work on a novel that eventually became *The Way of All Flesh,* but since he continued to work on it off and on until 1883, the books he wrote and published in the meantime will be considered first. Four of these books deal with Darwinism.[15]

Although Darwin had added to the third edition (1861) of *The Origin* a historical sketch briefly tracing the course of evolutionary theorizing through the ages, Butler for some time did not discover these previous thinkers and tended to assume that "natural selection" (Huxley's phrase, not Darwin's) and "evolution" were synonymous terms. His *Press* articles and "The Book of the Machines" in *Erewhon* had dealt with the paradoxical implications of "survival of the fittest": that if organisms develop by chance variations, either they are machines, nothing but levers and chemical processes, or machines are organisms and can develop the ability to think and plan that living beings seem to possess. He had brought out in both his *Press* articles and in "The Book of the Machines" the surprising and shocking implications of these two possible views. But his mind kept gnawing away at the problem of providing some more believable and less mechanical explanation of organic development than mere chance, worked upon by natural selection or survival of the fittest. How are successes, achieved in the struggle for survival, maintained, developed, and handed on? In a flash of what seemed to him great discovery he conceived the idea of "unconscious memory" to introduce a meaningful mental agent into the blind Darwinian mechanical process. He set forth this idea in *Life and Habit.*

Having done this, Butler turned to the background of evolutionary theory and in daily visits to the British Museum, begun in 1877, he read and absorbed the predecessors Darwin had mentioned in his historical sketch but had failed to discuss in any detail. This he did to buttress and support his "discovery" of the unconscious and to provide background that would win his unconscious memory theory a hearing. To his surprise, he found that both Comte Georges Louis Leclerc de Buffon and the Chevalier de Lamarck had had what now seemed to him a more plausible theory of evolution than the Darwinian one. He wrote *Evolution, Old and New* (1879) to make this point clear. Getting little response from the scientific world, he then followed with a more polemical defense of his theory and a direct attack on Charles Darwin in *Unconscious Memory* (1880), and completed his forays into evolutionary speculations with *Luck, or Cunning?* (1886) by underlining his conviction that if there is any purpose in evolutionary development as we now observe it taking place, as there seems to be, purpose or cunning must have been present from the start.

What Butler was trying to do was to stem the tide of meaninglessness with which the theory of natural selection seemed to be inundating life because Darwin refused to consider the operation in evolution of any force except that of chance variations. Butler was to become one of the most dogged, perceptive, and forceful opponents of Darwinism in the nineteenth century; he brought to bear on the underpinnings and implications of the new scientific orthodoxy, as no one else had done, a subtle verbal analysis, and, unlike the religious fundamentalists of his era, he was not to rely upon authority and accepted tradition for his argument. Instead, he used the sharp rapier of a practiced mind to reveal that Darwinism did not explain what people usually thought it explained: namely, why organic changes occur, and how they are transmitted. He was able to show with a kind of savage glee that the scientific bigwigs of his day, with their philosophical clumsiness and lack of subtlety, constantly smuggled into their arguments words that implied purposiveness and memory, both of which he desired to present forthrightly. He thus brought down upon himself opprobrium, vituperation, and the deadening silence of the "people who are above suspicion."[16] No one believed that the "comic writer" who had produced such puzzling books as *Erewhon* and *The Fair Haven* could have anything serious to say, and indeed his suggestions are brilliant metaphors rather than scientifically supported evidence. But even among biologists, one writer tells us, "There will always be a few who feel in their bones a sneaking sympathy with Samuel Butler's scepticism."[17] Basil Willey likewise states: "There have always been a few who have thought, or hoped, that Lamarck and Butler would turn out to be in some sense right after all."[18] In another passage he adds: "It may be that modern genetics and biochemistry will some day discover the mechanism behind the process thus metaphorically described by Lamarck; at any rate, an uneasy feeling has often recurred, in others beside Butler and Shaw, that Lamarck may have been in some sense right after all."[19]

It is hard to understand the dynamic outpouring of energy that led Butler to write and to publish four large books in nine years. One might think that he was hoping to benefit from the increasing public interest in Darwinism, but since his books were designed to antagonize Darwin's growing following rather than to appeal to it, this seems unlikely. And also since he did not cast his books into standard scientific form and did not report detailed research beyond commonsense speculations, it would seem that even he must have known that he would get no serious attention from the scientific world. There is also the possibility, as several have surmised, that he had a profound need to attack father figures and those in authority.[20] But most likely, as he himself believed, his insights so overwhelmed him that he could not refuse to develop and express them. He was elucidating what people then and since have been perfectly willing to call "instinct" (scientists still use this vague and ill-defined term) by adding a psychic component to it and calling it "unconscious memory." He was among the first to get a glimpse of the power and potentiality of the unconscious world later so spectacularly explored by Sigmund Freud.[21]

Life and Habit

Butler had written a key passage about inherited memory in June 1874, shortly after his arrival in Montreal (*Unconscious Memory*, 20), but had not grasped the full implications of his own idea at that time. Then in 1876 the power of this idea assailed him forcefully, and he experienced the excitement and terror of the hero of *Erewhon* as he crosses from one world into another. Although at first he thought the idea might be merely a satiric twist, by February 1876, he tells us: "I had gripped my meaning, and knew it to be sound."[22] As he worked deeper into the concept of inherited memory, he found: "The theory frightens me—it is so far-reaching and subversive—it oppresses me and I take panics that there cannot really be any solid truth in it . . . do what I can, I am oppressed and frightened."[23] Writing the book literally took his breath away: "I kept wanting to take a long breath, and was quite unable to do so. . . . It was a full year after *Life and Habit* was published before I righted myself."[24] For the very first time he was truly convinced that he had answered the questions left unanswered by Darwin of how organic change is handed on, once achieved, and could lay to rest the paradox of man as machine or machine as man that had assailed him since his New Zealand days. His concern now was how to present his findings effectively so that others could see their validity too.

In *Life and Habit* Butler explored the role of the unconscious as revealed in the uncanny operation of memory. He noted that the things we know best are the things of which we are least conscious, as exemplified by the accomplished pianist who can play a difficult composition while chatting with a friend. In all of this he was on the same track of investigation as that later pursued by Freud. His aim, though, was not to explore normal or abnormal behavior but to unlock the riddle of evolution. He was most interested in ascertaining how individuals travel in the paths of their forefathers without conscious thought about what they are doing, and his approach is disarmingly simple, and his analysis is full of humor. He says right at the start: "I have no wish to instruct, and not much to be instructed; my aim is simply to entertain and interest the numerous class of people who, like myself, know nothing of science, but who enjoy speculating and reflecting (not too deeply) upon the phenomena around them. I have therefore allowed myself a loose rein, to run on with whatever came uppermost" (1). But actually Butler came to regard his theory as extremely important, so much so that he wrote to Francis Darwin: "Pitch into it and into me by all means. You cannot do me a greater service than to bundle me neck and crop out of my present position."[25]

In *Life and Habit* Butler's intuition moves to the borderline of the known and explores the enigmatic and equivocal operation of the mind. Most readers would grant what he says about the superficial aspects of this subject, but a perceptive reader will follow him into the deeper implications. The better we know something, he argues, the less conscious we are of knowing it; then it follows that only those things that we do without any consciousness at all are completely known. Thus "perfect knowledge and perfect ignorance" become "extremes which meet . . . so that the mere fact of conscious knowing or willing implies the presence of more or less novelty and doubt" (15).

In light of these precepts, the kleptomaniac is the only perfect thief, and the greatest hypocrite is the man who "has left off knowing that he is a hypocrite" (18). The man who says: "My belief is that a widely extended good practice must be founded upon Christian doctrine" is less sure of himself than one who says "The Church of England . . . is in fact a church *sui generis,* yielding in point of dignity, purity, and decency of its doctrines, establishment, and ceremonies, to no congregation of Christians in the world" (20–21). This latter statement, Butler says, "is the language of faith, compelled by the exigencies of the occasion to be for a short time conscious of its own existence, but surely very little likely to become so to the extent of feeling the need of any assistance from reason" (21). The same argument holds for infidelity: "It is the unconscious unbeliever who is the true infidel" (21). As an example, he cites the man who asked the Almighty to "change our rulers *as soon as possible*" (22).

In *Life and Habit* Butler explores the revelations of unconscious humor, quoting, for example, Bacon's remark that " 'Reading good books on morality is a little flat and dead.' " He points out that this "is pregnant with painful inferences concerning Bacon's moral character," since it shows that he must have been "reading good books of morality," and yet did not "feel the loathing for further discourses upon the matter which honest people commonly feel now" (23, 24). Thus also when we hear one person praise another for earnestness we feel "that the praiser's attention must have been arrested by sincerity, as by something more or less unfamiliar to himself" (24). He concludes: "It is only those who are ignorant and uncultivated who can know anything at all in a proper sense of the words. . . . Knowledge is in an inchoate state as long as it is capable of logical treatment" (24–25). Thomas Hardy, in *The Return of the Native,* in contrasting the suffering of Clem Yeobright, the sophisticated intellectual, with the instinctive happiness of the peasants on Egdon Heath, was exploring the same paradox; but the conclusions Hardy drew were pessimistic, while Butler rejoices in men of intuitive good sense—his Ydgrunites and his Towneleys.

The paradox of the relation between conscious and unconscious knowledge is again well expressed in the following example: "Dog-fanciers tell us that performing dogs never carry their tails; such dogs have eaten of the tree of knowledge, and are convinced of sin accordingly—they know that they know things, in respect of which, therefore, they are no longer under grace, but under the law, and they have yet so much grace left as to be ashamed. So with the human clever dog; he may speak with the tongues of men and angels, but so long as he knows that he knows, his tail will droop" (31). Should we suggest to the Venus de Milo that she learn to read? "Beauty is but knowledge perfected and incarnate. . . . It is not knowledge, then, that is incompatible with beauty; there cannot be too much knowledge, but it must have passed through many people who it is to be feared must be both ugly and disagreeable, before beauty or grace will have anything to say to it" (32).

Knowing and Willing

The next step in his argument is to include *willing* in the same category as *knowing*. Here he makes an obvious parallel when he says: "we do not will anything utterly and without . . . hesitation, till we have lost sight of the fact that we are exercising our will" (36). Butler finds two classes of actions: those like eating, which must be learned, though they are learned easily, signifying a great readiness to learn them since so many of our ancestors have learned them; and those like swallowing, which we can do at birth because the knowledge is deeper in us and goes back through more generations than the knowledge of eating. We have invented the word *heredity* to explain the ability of the newborn baby to swallow, to digest, to oxidize the blood without previous practice; but the word merely names a difficulty and does not explain it, even though since Butler's day our knowledge of the DNA molecule reveals the mechanism of heredity. It does not tell us how the molecular arrangements that provide heredity are themselves established. "Why," Butler asks, "should heredity enable a creature to dispense with the experience which we see to be necessary in all other cases before difficult operations can be performed successfully?" (41). The answer, he suggests, lies in supposing "the continuity of life and sameness between living beings, whether plants or animals, and their descendants, to be far closer than we have hitherto believed" (41). The fact that "we are *most conscious of, and have most control over,* such habits as speech, the upright position, the arts and sciences . . . which are acquisitions peculiar to the human race," and "are *most unconscious of, and have least control over,* our digestion, which we have in common even with our invertebrate ancestry" (42) goes far to prove this. Someday, after many more ages have passed, we will read and write as instinctively as we now circulate our blood. But if human records should be lost, it will take another Harvey to discover that we do so.

Having established a seemingly plausible case for the actions of unconscious knowledge and will, Butler draws further conclusions that have become less meaningful since the discovery of the molecular basis in DNA of stored hereditary information. He argues that the skill of the unborn chicken in getting out of its shell shows that unborn beings possess an uncanny knowledge of what they want and of the means for getting it: the unborn chick grows a tip on its bill with which to peck a hole in its shell exactly as though it knew that such was necessary for it to be born. This unconscious knowledge is perfect because it is the result of infinite practice on the part of the chicken's ancestors; or, we might say, the skill it exhibits shows that *"it is the same chicken which makes itself over and over again"* (61). Butler continues: "What is the discovery of the laws of gravitation as compared with the knowledge which sleeps in every hen's egg upon a kitchen shelf?" (62). "We have established," he concludes, "that all living creatures which show any signs of intelligence, must certainly each one have already gone through the embryonic stages an infinite number of times, or they could no more have achieved the intricate process of self-development unconsciously, than they could play the piano unconsciously without any previous knowledge of the instrument" (63). There is, then, no single stopping point in considering what constitutes personal identity. Each individual is, in a sense, identical with the primordial cell from which he sprang. Yes, in a sense, but this denial of personal identity flies in the face of the commonsense view of reality Butler never tired of championing.

He also scrutinizes personal identity from the point of view of a given moment, and he discovers that here too the boundaries are far from sharp. We are not only ourselves, but also the sum total of all the influences upon us. "Who shall draw the line," he asks, "between the parasites which are part of us, and the parasites which are not part of us?" (87). Are we not as much "processes of [our] wives or nearest relations" (85–86) as of the corpuscles of our blood? "There is no line possible. Everything melts away into everything else" (87). He proceeds to deduce: "It would appear, then, as though 'we,' 'our souls,' or 'selves,' or 'personalities' . . . are but the *consensus* and full flowing stream of countless sensations and impulses on the part of our tributary souls or 'selves' " (89). And, he asks: "Is it possible to avoid imagining that we may be ourselves atoms, undesignedly combining to form some vaster being, though we are utterly incapable of perceiving that any such being exists?" (90).

These literary excursions, which fit into many Victorian speculations, help to explain why most of the scientific community, which insists on carefully drawn lines, rejects the work of Samuel Butler.

Still, the possibilities of the lines of thought opened up in *Life and Habit* continue to intrigue, and Butler pursues them one after another like an accomplished composer creating variations on a theme. He considers, for example, that a hen is an egg's way of making another egg: "We see an egg, A, which evidently knows its own meaning perfectly well, and we know that a twelvemonth ago there were two other such eggs, B and C, which have now disappeared, but from which we know A to have been so continuously developed as to be part of the present form of their identity. . . . It would seem, then, unreasonable to deny that A is only B and C come back, with such modifications as they may have incurred since their disappearance" (110).

Similarly, Butler considers what happens to an individual put into surroundings for which its memories have not prepared it, as, for example, a grain of corn put into a hen's stomach. The shock is so great that the grain forgets its own memories and adopts those of the hen, and "there is no such persecutor of grain, as another grain when it has fairly identified itself with a hen" (112). Thus Butler says: "The great question between vast masses of living organism is simply this: 'Am I to put you into a position with which your forefathers have been unfamiliar, or are you to put me into one about which my own have been in like manner ignorant?' Man is only the dominant animal on the earth, because he can, as a general rule, settle this question in his own favour" (113–14).

Again, Butler analyzes the odd ways in which memory operates, showing how long-forgotten chains of recollection can be activated by a chance occurrence, and how often the things we remember best, such as which leg to put first into our trousers on arising, are those we are so unconscious of as not to know that we know them. In like fashion, the caterpillar remembers exactly what to do in each stage of its varied existence. Finally, the infertility of hybrids is obviously explainable by the incompatibility of the divergent memories supplied to the embryo by the parents. He quotes from Darwin a description of the failure of five hundred crossbred eggs to mature, and he comments: "No wonder the poor creatures died, distracted as they were by the internal tumult of conflicting memories. . . . Five hundred creatures puzzled to death is not a pleasant subject for contemplation" (142).

Darwin had cited the example of neuter insects as evidence that the "well-known doctrine of inherited habit as advanced by Lamarck"[26] was untenable. Butler seizes on this and explains at length how his memory theory can account even for the activities of neuter insects. A passage based on an extended analogy exemplifies the literary vividness and humor of his reasoning and shows why he is so exasperating to the scientific brotherhood, unused as it always has been to figurative language:

Or take, again, the constitution of the Church of England. The bishops are the spiritual queens, the clergy are the neuter workers. They differ widely in structure (for dress must be considered as a part of structure), in the delicacy of the food they eat and the kind of house they inhabit, and also in many of their instincts, from the bishops, who are their spiritual parents. Not only this, but there are two distinct kinds of neuter workers—priests and deacons; and of the former there are deans, archdeacons, prebends, canons, rural deans, vicars, rectors, curates, yet all spiritually sterile. In spite of this sterility, however, is there anyone who will maintain that the widely differing structures and instincts of these castes are not due to inherited spiritual habits? Still less will he be inclined to do so when he reflects that by such slight modification of treatment as consecration and endowment any one of them can be rendered spiritually fertile. (194–95).

The reader should not be misled by the humor of passages like these. Butler was very serious indeed in his criticism of the theory of natural selection, for he pointed out that it amounts "to little more than to a statement of the fact that when variations have arisen they will accumulate" (203). Perhaps the problem is that Butler as a literary artist really believed that by appealing to imagination, insight, complex vision, and by using the gifts of metaphor, simile, hyperbole, satire he could reach the hearts and minds of a growingly scientific world of believers in hard facts established by precise laboratory procedures and precise rules of writing. But there was really no way of doing this. The plain fact was that Darwin refused, and science itself still refuses, to address the question of why variations occur. Butler felt that he must get "behind the back of 'natural selection,' which is rather a shield and hindrance to our perception of our own ignorance than an explanation of what these causes are" (203). Throughout *Life and Habit* he is indeed trying to get "behind the back of" conventional modes of thinking, and his vivid exposition of the ways of doing so has remarkable power to guide the sympathetic reader. *Life and Habit* is one of the most provocative books to come out of Victorian England.

Butler was really fighting for the view that the world contained more than blind chance. He was maintaining that natural selection is not an adequate explanation or guiding principle and that biology must have a vitalistic theory if it is to have any theory at all. To dramatize his point, he cites the leaf moth, which can imitate leaves in all states of disease and decay. He writes: "I can no more believe that these artificial fungi in which the moth arrays itself are due to the accumulation of minute, perfectly blind, and unintelligent variations, than I can believe that the artificial flowers which a woman wears in her hat can have got there without design; or that a detective puts on plain clothes without the slightest intention of making his victim think that he is not a policeman" (221). Later he adds, ". . . than I can believe that a mousetrap or a steam-engine is the result of the accumulation of blind fortuitous variations in a creature called man, which creature has never wanted either mousetraps or steam-engines, but has had a sort of promiscuous tendency to make them" (222).

Butler concludes his volume *Life and Habit,* as he had other pieces before, by calling it tentative, a sketch or design for further endeavor "in which I hope to derive assistance from the criticisms which this present volume may elicit" (240). He likens it to a work of art, the spirit of which is more important than detailed accuracy. But, he adds: "I am in very serious earnest, perhaps too much so, from the first page of my book to the last" (249). He tells us:

I saw, as it were, a pebble upon the ground, with a sheen that pleased me; taking it up, I turned it over and over for my amusement, and found it always grow brighter and brighter the more I examined it. At length I became fascinated, and gave loose rein to self-illusion. The aspect of the world seemed changed; the trifle which I had picked up idly had proved to be a talisman of inestimable value, and had opened a door through which I caught glimpses of a strange and interesting transformation. . . . Will the reader bid me wake with him to a world of chance and blindness? Or can I persuade him to dream with me of a more living faith than either he or I had as yet conceived as possible? As I have said, reason points remorselessly to an awakening, but faith and hope still beckon to the dream." (249–50).

From reviewers or from the professional world Butler received little assistance in appraising his theory. The *Athenaeum,*[27] although admitting that the book contained "serious and important scientific truth," suspected a hoax and took Butler to task for his untenable view of reason. The *Contemporary Review*[28] said: "The work contains much shrewd sense in a whimsical form"; but it criticized Butler, on his own principles, for emphasizing his earnestness, and it objected to his attacks on Darwin. The *Westminster Review*[29] advised the general reader and those interested in evolution to read the book which, it avowed, contains "much food for reflection in its pages," and it went on to say that "the incisive touches of the satirist are combined with the more sober suggestions of the scientific critic." Although the *Saturday Review*[30] called the main thesis of *Life and Habit* "a suggestion towards the completion of the Darwinian theory . . . showing the line which future contributions may take," it accused Butler of falling "into the very fallacy of [von] Hartmann," and of being "on the high road to chimaera-land." The *Spectator*[31] likewise attacked Butler's conception of the unconscious, saying that we could never have proof of the existence of the unconscious if it is really unconscious. Alfred Russell Wallace, co-discoverer with Darwin of the "survival of the fittest" principle, writing in *Nature,* concluded that "Though we can at present only consider the work as a most ingenious and paradoxical speculation, it may yet afford a clue to some of the deepest mysteries of the organic world."[32] But in spite of such passages of serious criticism, no one took the trouble to bundle Butler "neck and crop out of [his] present position."

Chapter Four
Defending His Position

While working on *Life and Habit*, Butler had read the works of Darwin's immediate predecessors and had been amazed to find that they had made the same points as Darwin, but had also provided what he thought was a believable explanation for the "fortuitous variations" Darwin's theory depended upon. He failed to notice or forgot that Darwin's theory of natural selection was supported by a vast amount of empirical evidence not provided by Buffon or Lamarck, and that Darwin, in spite of ambiguities of language and some vacillating, did not really attempt to explain why or how variations occur.

Evolution, Old and New

In his next book, *Evolution, Old and New* (1879), Butler attempted to establish that Charles Darwin was not as original as people thought and as he himself seemed to claim (since his historical sketch was, Butler thought, all too "brief but imperfect")[1] and that the work of both Buffon and Lamarck fitted perfectly into the "unconscious memory" theory of *Life and Habit*.

Butler opened *Evolution, Old and New* by stating as forcefully as he could the reasons for believing in a purposefulness in evolutionary development—a purposefulness in the organism itself, not in a divine creator who stands outside the organic world. The existence of rudimentary organs and of the process of embryonic recapitulation, he argued, supports his view, since it is unlikely that an all-powerful designer would see fit to retain so much that was apparently useless. He quoted at length from William Paley's *Natural Theology*, agreeing enthusiastically with the evidence for design that Paley cited. Butler disagreed, however, that this evidence proved the existence of a forming agent other than the organism itself. "What is commonly conceived of as direct creation by God is moved back to a time and space inconceivable in their remoteness," he wrote, "while the aim and design so obvious in nature are shown to be still at work around us, growing ever busier and busier, and advancing from day to day both in knowledge and power" (35). He then complained that "Mr. Darwin . . . tangled and obscured what his predecessors had made in great part, if not wholly, plain" (36–37).

In Buffon, Butler discovered a man he could heartily admire. He became convinced that the exigencies of the era had forced Buffon to conceal his real meaning behind protective irony. He complimented Buffon for his skill in doing this: "What he did was to point so irresistibly in the right direction, that a reader of any intelligence should be in no doubt as to the road he ought to take, and then to contradict himself so flatly as to reassure those who would be shocked by a truth for which they were not yet ready" (72).[2] Butler recognized this device in Buffon because he himself had used it in *The Fair Haven*. Buffon could also write entertaining passages, and "he looked to these parts of his work to keep the whole alive till the time should come when the philosophical side of his writings should be understood and appreciated" (74). Commenting further on Buffon's irony, Butler remarks: "Complaint, then, against an ironical writer on the score that he puzzles us, is a complaint against irony itself; for a writer is not ironical unless he puzzles. He should not puzzle unless he believes that this is the best manner of making his reader understand him in the end" (96).

Evolution, Old and New shows by apt quotation that Buffon did not believe in final causes, for he realized that nature could not tolerate rudimentary organs while working in the light of a clear design. The quotations also show that Buffon recognized inner feelings as a modifying factor and that he was aware of the effect of environment in controlling the spread of living forms. Butler speaks admiringly of Buffon's contempt for science—for its giving of names to things too unimportant to be named and for its assuming that naming is synonymous with explaining. He also discovers to his delight that Buffon had entertained the notion of personal identity through the ages. " 'Man,' " he translates Buffon as saying, " 'and especially educated man, is no longer a single individual. . . . having discovered the divine art of fixing their thoughts so that they can transmit them to their posterity, [men] become, as it were, one and the same people with their descendants' " (132).

In his discussion of Dr. Erasmus Darwin (1731–1802), which follows his study of Buffon, Butler points out that Dr. Darwin believed that individuals are " 'elongations of the parents' " (174); but since he referred instinct to imitation, rather than to memory, he failed to anticipate Butler's own view. Yet Dr. Darwin admitted that "instinct is only reason become habitual" (179). In his discussion of mating he recognized a "survival-of-the-fittest" factor: " 'The final cause of this contest among the males,' " Dr. Darwin wrote, " 'seems to be *that the strongest and most active animal should propagate the species, which should thence become improved*' " (200). Butler remarks on this: "There have been two factors in modification; the one provides variations, the other accumulates them" (201). Dr. Darwin gives an account of the beaks of different species of birds " 'all [of] which seem to have been gradually produced during many generations *by the perpetual endeavour of the creature to supply the want of food, and to have been delivered to their posterity with constant improvement of them for the purposes required*' " (202).

Although Butler finds less in Lamarck than in Buffon and Dr. Darwin to please him, he is particularly anxious to rescue Lamarck from neglect because he had been penniless and had had no group around him who could defend his name, thus giving him a kind of kinship with Butler himself, who at this time was in serious financial straits and certainly had no one to defend his name. That Lamarck was aware of the part played by environment in evolution is shown by the following quotation: " 'In consequence of the extremely rapid rate of increase of the smaller, and especially of the most imperfect, animals, their numbers would become so great as to prove injurious to the conservation of breeds, and to the progress already made towards more perfect organization, unless nature had taken precautions to keep them down within certain fixed limits which she cannot exceed' " (247). This passage, Butler says, contains all the survival of the fittest "necessary for Lamarck's purpose. . . . Nothing therefore can be more at variance with the truth than to represent Lamarck and the other early evolutionists as ignoring the struggle for existence and the survival of the fittest" (247–48).

After discussing the theories of Patrick Matthew, Etienne and Isidore Geoffroy, and Herbert Spencer, all of whom had preceded Darwin, Butler compares the old and new views. Both views maintain that animals and plants vary, and both hold that variations are transmitted to offspring. But the old view finds the cause of variation in changing conditions of existence, and in "varying needs arising from" (298) these changes, whereas "Mr. Darwin . . . repeatedly avows ignorance, and profound ignorance, concerning the causes of those variations" (299), though he admits the effect of use or disuse, and regards survival of the fittest as "the most important but not the exclusive means of modification" (301). Butler again points out, however, that "natural selection cannot be considered a cause of variation" (304), as Darwin frequently implies that it is; and he says that therefore the *Origin of Species* has no raison de'être, that it is "no less a piece of intellectual sleight-of-hand than Paley's *Natural Theology*" (305). The last three chapters of *Evolution, Old and New* are a brilliant display of Butler's power to analyze careless and confusing statements. But they overlook the fact that in spite of his confusing use of language, Darwin simply did not believe that science could address the question of why variations occur.

The reviewers were outraged by *Evolution, Old and New*, especially by its criticism of Darwin; and, like *Life and Habit*, it was not given a serious examination. It was said to be full of fallacies and verbal quibbles, not to leave "a single clear idea of what it has been driving at." Butler was called crotchety, and he was advised to return to the writing of fiction.[3] Alfred R. Wallace, however, discussed the book more seriously in a leading article in *Nature*,[4] calling it interesting and useful, and stating that Butler's hypothesis, supported by the historical background he provides, forms "an important and even a necessary supplement to the theory advocated by Mr. Darwin." He agreed with Butler's evaluation of Buffon, but he refused in conclusion to find any force in Butler's attack on Darwin.

The Quarrel with Darwin

In November 1879 a book entitled *Erasmus Darwin* was published with a preliminary notice by Charles Darwin. In this preface Darwin said that the body of the book was a translation from the German of an article by Ernest Krause which had appeared in *Kosmos* before *Evolution, Old and New* was written.[5] When Butler read the new work, he was amazed to find Krause stating in his conclusion that "Erasmus Darwin's system was in itself a most significant first step in the path of knowledge which his grandson has opened up for us; but the wish to revive it at the present day, as has actually been seriously attempted, shows a weakness of thought and a mental anachronism which no one can envy." Butler also found quotations from Buffon using the exact wording of his own translations from the French. There were other evidences that the work was a covert attack upon him written after *Evolution, Old and New* had appeared.

After hastily learning enough German to serve his purpose, Butler compared the translation with the German original and found that much material, including the final six pages, had been added. The work was thus not what Darwin's preface said that it was—a translation of an article written before *Evolution, Old and New*.[6] Butler immediately wrote to Charles Darwin for an explanation. Darwin replied that alterations in translations were "so common a practice that it never occurred to me to state that the article had been modified."[7] This explanation did not satisfy Butler, who, having informed Darwin that he was going to do so, proceeded to air the matter in a letter to the *Athenaeum*.[8] Darwin wished to answer this letter. He wanted to point out that, when he first wrote to Butler, he had forgotten that the printer had inadvertently omitted from the book a statement that the text was a revision. Though his son, Francis Darwin, felt that Darwin should reply, Thomas Henry Huxley advised against any rejoinder.[9] "A clever and unscrupulous man like Mr. Butler," Darwin wrote to Huxley, indicating his own fearfulness, "would be sure to twist whatever I may say against me."[10] Some months later, after *Unconscious Memory* had appeared with an account of the whole matter, Francis Darwin again wished his father to make a public statement. This time it was Leslie Stephen who advised against it.

Thus Butler was never to learn that the whole affair had originated in an error compounded by forgetfulness and bad advice. At the very least, his anger was justified, if only by the cowardliness of those who told the aging Darwin to refuse an explanation that could have been so simply provided. In 1904 Francis Darwin wrote his sister that he had omitted the controversy when he edited his father's letters, but added "I now think he [Butler] had some cause of complaint, though he entirely lost his head and behaved abominably."[11]

Ralf Norrman remarks that "Butler certainly felt persecuted much of the time: but then, objectively speaking, he often was persecuted."[12] Others have been more harsh on him for his frontiersmanlike quarrels, maintaining that they are paranoid and a continuing projection of his troubles with his father: substitute fathers like Charles Darwin were necessary to him, they believe.[13] These views have psychological validity but tend to overlook the objective facts of the case: Butler was sure that his "unconscious memory" theory was a great discovery, just as he later came to feel that he had made great discoveries about Homer, Shakespeare, and Italian artists; he was infuriated that the scientific world refused to give his theory serious attention. If he was wrong, why did not someone prove that he was wrong? He failed to understand that science cannot easily deal with the unconscious and with purposiveness. His position was to a certain extent not unlike that of Sigmund Freud in the early years of his explorations, except that Freud already had professional standing and continued to develop empirical evidence to support his theorizing until his work was more widely understood.

Unconscious Memory

Butler had become convinced that "people who are above suspicion," namely, the scientists, would stop at nothing to secure their positions, and in true frontier spirit he wanted to "give old Darwin the best warming I can manage to give him—and I think I shall manage a pretty hot one."[14]

Unconscious Memory begins with an account of what the *Origin of Species* had meant to its first readers who did not probe its exact meaning carefully enough to discover that it did not fully explain what it appeared to explain. After a brief résumé of his own writings on evolution, Butler shows that Darwin carefully covered his tracks and left the impression that no major work had been done with the theory of evolution before his own. Much of the analysis in this part of his book is based on a subtle reading between the lines and upon inferences regarding Darwin's hidden motives. With skillful citation of texts and analysis of grammatical vagueness, Butler cuts through the complexities and makes out a good case for his thesis that Darwin appears to explain why variations occur but does not actually do so.

The tone becomes progressively more angry and culminates in direct charges of unscrupulous behavior in the account of the *Kosmos* article affair. Butler had wanted a fight "according to the rules of the game," but he was convinced that his opponents were capable of hitting below the belt. There is little doubt that Huxley, the journalist and science reviewer Grant Allen, and Darwin himself failed to understand the issues at stake in the quarrel as clearly as Butler did. Nor did they appreciate the importance of meticulous honesty in dealing with an opponent and in presenting the history of an idea.

Butler was in a strong position and made the most of it in forensic style. In return, he received the bitterest treatment that can be handed out to a man looking for vigorous debate—silence. Or worse still, in our time, the insolent comments that he was an exhibitionist, a show-off, a neurotic. "Don't bother about me or my bad behavior," he might say to his modern detractors, were he alive today. "Bother about the issues. What do you say to them?"

That Butler never regarded his quarrel with Darwin as a passing affair is shown by his request to Streatfeild shortly before his death that *Unconscious Memory*, the most quarrelsome book he had ever written, should be reissued in a new edition (xiv). "When I thought," he had written in that book,

of Buffon, of Dr. Erasmus Darwin, of Lamarck, and even of the author of the *Vestiges of Creation*, to all of whom Mr. Darwin had dealt the same measure which he was now dealing to myself; when I thought of these great men, now dumb, who had borne the burden and heat of the day, and whose laurels had been filched from them; of the manner, too, in which Mr. Darwin had been abetted by those who should have been the first to detect the fallacy which had misled him; of the hotbed of intrigue which science has now become; of the disrepute into which we English must fall as a nation if such practices as Mr. Darwin had attempted in this case were to be tolerated;—when I thought of all this, I felt that though prayers for the repose of dead men's souls might be unavailing, yet a defence of their work and memory, no matter against what odds, might avail the living, and resolved that I would do my utmost to make my countrymen aware of the spirit now ruling among those whom they delight to honour. (53–54)

After setting his case before the public, Butler goes on in *Unconscious Memory* to present the theory of a German scientist, Ewald Hering, who in 1870 had read to the Imperial Academy of Sciences at Vienna a statement of his thesis that heredity is linked to memory and that memory can be traced to minute vibrations common to all matter and thus is a universal property. In general, Butler insisted on his right to stand on common sense and not to raise questions that were too remotely speculative; but Hering's suggestions intrigued him because they seemed to provide a basis for his own views and thus he found them a valuable addition to his *Life and Habit* theory. In the section on "Vibrations" in Jones's edition of the *Note-Books* Butler explores the matter further. Characteristically, he says: "I was alarmed by the suggestion and fathered it upon Professor Hering who never, that I can see, meant to say anything of the kind, but I forced my view on him, as it were, by taking hold of a sentence or two in his lecture" (61).

In *Unconscious Memory* Butler also presents an extract from von Hartmann's *Philosophy of the Unconscious* which he translated for this occasion.[15] He had been accused of falling into "the fallacy of von Hartmann" in his use of unconscious memory in *Life and Habit*; but, on studying the German author, he found the unconscious conceived of as a mysterious, clairvoyant agency so far from the simple idea that he had himself presented that it repelled him. He rejected it emphatically. His notes on various passages in the text are an acute analysis of the basic differences between his view and the German scientist's, and the points he makes reveal also, we imagine, what reservations he might have concerning the Freudian unconscious were he alive today. One telling observation he makes is that instinctive or unconscious knowledge is always the result of long-repeated, conscious effort; it is not something generically different from and below consciousness. At the end of his book he discusses the reasons why a memory theory is called for and why a purely mechanistic view will not suffice to explain the actions of organic beings. He also suggests that there must be incipient traces of mind even in the inorganic world. Without any matter, there would be no mind, he says, and, without mind, no matter.

Butler hoped that his direct attack on Darwin would get him a hearing, but he was disappointed. Very few reviewers paid any attention to *Unconscious Memory*. The *Athenaeum*[16] complained of "the gradual decline in the literary qualities" of Butler's work. George J. Romanes, in a front-page article in *Nature*,[17] attacked Butler savagely, calling his book a "sorry exhibition" and Butler "an upstart ignoramus." Romanes continues: "A man who in the full light of Darwin's theory can deliberately return to the weak and beggarly elements of Lamarck— such a man shows only that in judgment he is still a child." Butler had to threaten legal action to force *Nature* to print a letter from him in which he reiterated that no one had yet answered his charges that Darwin had dealt in misrepresentation.[18] Romanes replied with further abuse.

It is interesting to note, however, that Butler did eventually win support. In 1884, when the *Athenaeum* reviewed Romanes's own work, *Mental Evolution in Animals,* it took Romanes severely to task for not even mentioning that Butler had originated a theory that Romanes now called his own.[19] "We have previously called attention to Mr. Butler's views as deserving a hearing by professional biologists. . . . This attention has now been paid to Mr. Butler's work, but it must be regretted that more attention has not been paid to Mr. Butler's feelings and to Mr. Butler's rights over the valuable suggestions he has made to students of descent which, it would seem from the book before us, are hence-forth to be adopted as an integral part of Darwinistic doctrine." When Romanes replied defending himself,[20] the reviewer pointed out that between 1859 and 1883 in which latter year "Mr. Romanes

devotes more than half of his treatment of instinct to inherited memory,"
Mr. Butler had produced *Life and Habit.* "We therefore venture to
attribute the advance in Mr. Romanes' views about instinct to the
influence of Mr. Butler's work. . . . We still remain unconvinced by
Mr. Romanes' argument that he has satisfied the laws of literary
courtesy." The controversy continued with two more letters from Romanes, two from the reviewer, and one each from Professor Ray
Lankester, Herbert Spencer, and Butler himself.

In his discussion of Erasmus Darwin in *Evolution, Old and New*
Butler had said: "If his opponents, not venturing to dispute with him,
passed over one book in silence, he should have followed it up with
another, and another, and another, year by year, as Buffon and Lamarck
did; it is only thus that men can expect to succeed against vested
interests" (173). This was exactly what Butler was doing, although
hard-pressed financially and disappointed with each of his books that,
in turn, did not pay its own way. He kept hoping for a change in his
fortunes, however, and was fairly certain of eventual success (*Note-Books,*
6). It was not to come in his lifetime. At this time (1884) he wrote:
"My books are to me much the most important thing in life. They
are, in fact, 'me' much more than anything else."[21]

In March 1884 Butler published a volume of *Selections from Previous
Works, with Remarks on Romanes' "Mental Evolution in Animals"* and
"A Psalm of Montreal." Most reviewers ignored this new book, but the
Athenaeum[22] gave it a very favorable review. "These lively pages," it
said, "contain selections from works which are likely to exercise considerable influence on the most prominent doctrine of the age, the theory
of evolution. . . . Mr. Butler's service to students of descent consists
in the prominent way in which he has called attention to the causes,
as distinct from the fact, of evolution. . . . In identifying heredity and
memory Mr. Butler is on the highest wave of contemporary speculation."
The reviewer also remarked that Butler's literary style was "infinitely
superior to that of any other writer on evolution, with the exception
of Prof. Huxley."

Luck, or Cunning?

In spite of the poor sale of the *Selections*—it was the most unsuccessful
of all Butler's books—he reentered the evolutionary lists in 1887 with
a new volume, *Luck, or Cunning?* In his preface he says that he "became
more and more convinced," in the course of his writing, "that no

progress could be made towards a sounder view of the theory of descent until people came to understand what the late Mr. Charles Darwin's theory of natural selection amounted to. . . . Until the mindless theory of Charles-Darwinian natural selection was finally discredited, and a mindful theory of evolution was substituted in its place . . . my own theories could [not] stand much chance of being attended to" (xvii). Later he speaks of Darwin's "pitchforking . . . of mind out of the universe," but "so thickly had he gilded" the pill he was giving us "with descent with modification" that we "swallowed it without a murmur. . . . Indeed, we have even given life pensions to some of the most notable of these biologists" who supported Darwin, "I suppose to reward them for having hoodwinked us so much to our satisfaction" (6).

Butler is arguing again as he had always argued. Instead of seeing science as a specialized game played by specialized rules that only operate well when intangibles like intelligence are omitted from the reckoning, he is raising an outcry because, in his view, the game must be played with a wider reference. The point of view and the attitude one has are all-important, and the matter must first of all be fought out on the philosophical level.

Butler defends the right of a literary man to interest himself in a scientific subject. He defends the right of such a man to use facts he himself has not collected, just as an architect builds with stones he did not quarry. Yet he admits that his speculations have caused him much anxiety:

I must confess that I have found it [my theory] somewhat of a white elephant. It has got me into the hottest of hot water, made a literary Ishmael of me, lost me friends whom I have been sorry to lose, cost me a good deal of money, done everything to me, in fact, which a good theory ought not to do. Still, as it seems to have taken up with me, and no one else is inclined to treat it fairly, I shall continue to report its developments from time to time as long as life and health are spared me. Moreover, Ishmaels are not without their uses, and they are not a drug in the market just now. (14)

Butler obviously had a great deal of fun writing *Luck, or Cunning?* He traced down the shifting statements on instinct in the various editions of the *Origin of Species,* demonstrating that Darwin reversed himself again and again. He accused Darwin of never saying anything unequivocally because he always wanted to hedge. He presents telling examples of the "numerous, successive, slight alterations" Darwin made. He comments that in them "the working of Mr. Darwin's mind can be seen as though it were the twitchings of a dog's nose" (76).

Later in *Luck, or Cunning?* Butler returns to his Erewhonian argument that machines have a kind of life. Using the new conception of protoplasm as the basic living unit, he points out that many parts of the body, such as bones and nails, contain no protoplasm. Are we to call them dead? If not, then hammers and saws and hats and shoes which we habitually use are living too, though on a slightly more remote level than bones and nails. If so, then protoplasm may also be dead, since it contains substances like oxygen and hydrogen which are not protoplasm, and animals are machines. Indeed, he points out, the neo-Darwinian evolution (Charles Darwin's), by enthroning chance also enthrones mechanism; for there remains no legitimate function for thought and feeling: everything would go on just as it does if neither of these existed.

Butler is as certain as the Duke of Argyll,[23] whom he quotes, that Darwin's followers have attempted to read mind out of the universe; but worth noting is his disagreement with the Duke's remark that "a reign of terror" has been established. "It is hardly possible," Butler comments, "for any one to oppose the fallacy involved in the Charles-Darwinian theory of natural selection more persistently and unsparingly than I have done myself from the year 1877 onwards; naturally I have at times been very angrily attacked in consequence, and as a matter of business have made myself as unpleasant as I could in my rejoinders, but I cannot remember anything having been ever attempted against me which could cause fear in any ordinarily constituted person" (124).

After a lengthy presentation of further evidence that Darwin continually claimed the doctrine of survival of the fittest as his own and carefully avoided giving any credit to his predecessors, Butler examines Grant Allen's biography of Darwin. The fun he has with a passage from Allen is another good example of his method of attack. Allen had written of Darwin's view of the increments in brain power in contrast to Spencer's Lamarckian view: "I venture to think that the first way, if we look it clearly in the face, will seem to be practically unthinkable." Butler remarks:

I like our looking a 'way' which is 'practically unthinkable' 'clearly in the face.' I particularly like 'practically unthinkable.' I suppose we can think it in theory, but not in practice. I like almost everything Mr. Allen says or does; it is not necessary to go far in search of his good things; dredge up any bit of mud from him at random and we are pretty sure to find an oyster with a pearl in it, if we look it clearly in the face; I mean, there is sure to be something which will be at any rate 'almost' practically unthinkable. (189–90)

Luck, or Cunning? concludes with a discussion of Ray Lankester's attack on Lamarck and with a chapter "Per Contra" on Darwin's merits, wherein we are told that "Mr. Darwin played for his own generation, and he got in the very amplest measure the recognition which he endeavoured, as we all do, to obtain" (215).

If Butler hoped to make headway by writing "book after book" on evolution, he was disappointed. The *Athenaeum*[24] said it regretted "to see a mind of considerable power frittered away in ephemeral conflict," adding: "We have from the first acknowledged Mr. Butler's merits as an acute thinker on the problems of evolution." Some months later, when Butler wrote to the *Athenaeum* about another matter, he commented on the untruth of this statement: *Life and Habit* and *Unconscious Memory* had both been condemned in the *Athenaeum*.[25] The *Academy*[26] published a review by Grant Allen that considered none of the points Butler made but praised him in equivocal terms:

The hardest heart could not fail to be touched by the profound pathos of Mr. Samuel Butler's Op. 8. . . . In the first place, here is a work of consummate ingenuity, rare literary skill, and a certain happy vein of sardonic humor—a work pregnant with epigram, sparkling with wit, and instinct throughout with a powerful original fancy—flung out upon the world in the uncongenial guise of a scientific treatise. . . . He stands by himself, a paradoxer of the first water, hopeless and friendless, at least in the desert of the present generation. . . . He is made of the very stuff that heroes and martyrs and madmen are made of. . . . Filled with righteous wrath against the Frankenstein of his own brain [his view of Darwin], he goes forth now, a biological Quixote, to wage a holy war against the wicked giant he has laboriously invented for his personal vexation. . . . I have seldom read a more delightful and readable book, in its own way, than *Luck or Cunning*. It is a most valuable, original, and suggestive contribution to current evolutionary thought. The author of *Erewhon* has at bottom something to say.

At bottom, what Butler says and Grant Allen overlooks is that since Darwinism does nothing to explain why and how variations arise in the organic world and how they are transmitted, and for the most part refuses to address these questions, human beings, being aware of purposiveness in their own lives, should fill the gap by positing purposiveness from the very start. Then Butler proposes that unconscious memory will explain how the transmission of variations from generation to generation takes place. To do this he draws an analogy with the empirical fact that once human beings have mastered an art, it becomes unconscious. These two basic proposals, more literary than scientific, and defended with great verbal skill but not with laboratory experiments, have the merit of stirring thought and discussion, challenging the imagination, and at least attempting to fill the gaps that Darwin leaves unfilled. Science since Darwin's time has still only begun with its growing knowledge of genetics and of the mind to solve the two problems that so intrigued Samuel Butler.

Alps and Sanctuaries

The books on evolution represent Butler at the height of his literary power and constitute a very important part of his life's work. But at the same time that he was writing them he was engaged in other activities. In 1883, for example, Butler urged his friend Henry Festing Jones, who wanted to be a composer, to write in the manner of Handel, saying he was sure it could be done. Jones said to him: "Very well, then, do it and show it to me." When they met some days later at Heatherley's, Butler played a minuet he had composed to meet the challenge.[27] For the next two years the two worked together and in 1885 they published their *Gavottes, Minuets, Fugues, and Other Short Pieces for the Piano.* They took lessons in harmony and continued their collaboration in the composition of *Narcissus: a Cantata in the Handelian Form,* published in 1888. Some of Butler's contributions to these two works are delightful. Although written in the manner of Handel, they are more than merely imitative. In 1890 Butler wrote his sister May about the pleasure he felt on hearing of a girl who played his music to her friends and called it *"des oeuvres posthumes de Handel."*[28] After Butler's death Jones completed his part of the work on *Ulysses: an Oratorio* and published it in 1904. Butler's whole life was so steeped in Handel that one key to the understanding of his work can be found in the vigorous rhythms, melodic sweetness, and self-confident mastery of that great artist. One of his last requests as he lay dying was for the score of *Solomon.*

Even when hard pressed for money, Butler had insisted upon an annual vacation. He attributed his ability to keep going—despite multiform discouragements and the tension caused by his thinking beyond the confines of his era—to the fact that he made these breaks and fortified himself with impressions from another, healthier world.[29] One result of his travels was that in 1880 his publisher offered him £100 for an illustrated book about Italy,[30] if he would write one; and by mid-1881 Miss Savage was reading the completed manuscript with delight.[31] When the publisher did not like the work and rejected it, Butler published it in the fall at his own expense. This book, *Alps and Sanctuaries*—his most relaxed, casual work—is a tribute to his love for Italy, and a record of the thoughts that passed through his mind while he was in the land where so many of the theories of *Life and Habit* applied, where the inhabitants seemed to him to have achieved so much unconscious perfection. In many respects this work is the antithesis of *The Way of All Flesh,* that excoriating exposé of the evils wrought by self-conscious righteousness. *Alps and Sanctuaries* is also profusely illustrated with drawings Butler made of the places he wrote about, and it contains many passages from Handel that accompanied Butler just as they did the hero of *Erewhon.*

Since both Handel and Shakespeare made use of Italian material, Butler opens his volume with a comparison of them. He places Handel as much above Shakespeare for his unconscious power as Shakespeare is above other men. In discussing the St. Gotthard pass, entryway to Italy, Butler discourses on the importance of knowing what we really like and of not being led by fashion. We remember that in *The Way of All Flesh* (the passage was reconstructed by Streatfeild from Butler's notes) he makes fun of George Pontifex for his conventional raptures on viewing this pass (chapter 4). He has great faith in the creative ability of the mind that knows itself. How like William James's "Will to Believe" is the following: " 'the longing after immortality,' though not indeed much of an argument in favour of our being immortal at the present moment, is perfectly sound as a reason for concluding that we shall one day develop immortality, if our desire is deep enough and lasting enough" (7).

During the years Butler's thoughts about religion had mellowed from his New Zealand days when he had said he was renouncing Christianity altogether. He was now too aware of the problematic nature of human reason to wish any longer to be so sure of himself. He held views that, he felt, were not far from those held by his father and by every right-thinking man of the Church of England. As he had written in *Life and Habit,* the unintrospective beliefs of the Church, hallowed by long tradition, had more of truth in them than the new discoveries of the scientific pioneers. *Alps and Sanctuaries* conveys successfully much of the spirit of the Italian faith and is so full of respect for this traditional wisdom that it pleased many Catholic readers. Butler recalls an anecdote of an Italian woman in London who, missing the wayside shrines, said her prayers before a dentist's showcase; and he asks: "Which of us, indeed, does not sit contentedly enough upon chalk eggs at times?" (26). He then ascribes to the power of illusion much of the progress of mankind, and suggests that "the human intellect owes its superiority over that of the lower animals in great measure to the stimulus which alcohol has given to imagination" (27). In other words, worthy results can arise from unworthy causes. Thus with religion: The effect of their faith on the people of Italy argues that it must somehow be right after all, even if the probing intellect rejects it.

Butler speculates on the marvelous effect of crossing: of stimulating one way of being or line of thought by infusion from something different, but something not too different. He comments, too, on the growth in geometrical ratio of inventions, though observing that at each stage the inventors are "repudiated" and come "to a bad end" (42). Developments that previously took a thousand years have occurred in a hundred years; now they take ten years; soon they will take one year, then a tenth of a year, and so on. "It follows by an easy process of reasoning," he observes, "that, after another couple of hundred years or so, great sweeping changes should be made several times in an hour, or indeed in a second, or fraction of a second, till they pass unnoticed as the revolutions we undergo in the embryonic stages, or are felt simply as vibrations" (43). He concludes that the present time (1880) is the only "comfortable time for a man to live in. . . . The past was too slow, and the future will be too fast," thus taking a stand in favor of the very world that was so unreceptive to his own constant needling. From this he goes on to the idea that "science is rapidly reducing time and space to a very undifferentiated condition."

Butler indeed is acquiring a mellower understanding of the value of paradox in life. He purposely misquotes Tennyson: "There lives more doubt in honest faith" (48), and then calmly comments: "It is a bad sign for a man's peace in his own convictions when he cannot stand turning the canvas of his life occasionally upside down, or reversing it in a mirror, as painters do with their pictures" (50). But he builds no argument for revolt on this sad fact. However, he admires the Catholics in Italy especially because they can do this. He refers to the fool's mass of the medieval church and the gargoyles of Gothic cathedrals as evidence of the robustness of faith. "I would persuade all Jews, Mohammedans, Comtists, and freethinkers to turn high Anglicans, or better still, downright Catholics for a week in every year," he writes. "It is a great grief to me that there is no place where I can go among Mr. Darwin, Professors Huxley, Tyndall and Ray Lankester . . . as I can go among the Italian priests" (50–51).

Catholics, Butler believes, have the logical advantage over Protestants; but "reasonable people will look with distrust upon too much reason" (86). The important things in life—body, soul, money—are all taken on faith; faith and reason must go together, and are fused in what we call temper. "If it is asked, In what should a man have faith? . . . the answer is, [in] the current feeling among those whom he most looks up to—looking upon himself with suspicion if he is either among the foremost or the laggers" (88). This is Butler's conservatism, his Laodiceanism, his *surtout point de zèle*. But remembering his own creative life, we can believe that he did not misapply his doctrine. Indeed, he used only enough of the mood of *Alps and Sanctuaries* to keep himself alive.

These passages of speculation make up only a part of *Alps and Sanctuaries;* in the rest we get glimpses of Italian peasants and townspeople drawn with love, humor, and affection; of fascinating little villages nestled in the mountains above the Val Leventina; and of the author walking the trails in various seasons and weathers.

Among the most charming episodes of the book are the accounts Butler gives of his sojourns in out-of-the-way inns usually frequented only by Italians. Here his sensitivity comes into play, his ability to love and appreciate these people for their naturalness, which, he says, is as much above that of the English as the English are above the colonists.

A chapter on the decline of Italian art presents our author's view of the sources of artistic effectiveness. Priggishness—that is, a stilted adherence to conventions—, he says, is the besetting sin of Englishmen, which will last as long as Oxford and Cambridge universities last. Art in Italy has declined for priggish reasons—its contemporary painters are interested, not in painting out of love for a particular subject but in the desire to paint an academic picture. "The date of the opening of the Bolognese Academy coincides . . . with the complete decadence of Italian art" (126), he asserts. The trouble with the academic system is that it trains artists to study other men's work rather than nature. "As for the old masters," he adds, "the better plan would be never even to look at one of them, and to consign Raffaelle, along with Plato, Marcus Aurelius Antonius, Dante, Goethe, and two others, neither of them Englishmen, to limbo, as the Seven Humbugs of Christendom. While we are about it, let us leave off talking about 'art for art's sake.' Who is art, that it should have a sake?" (135).

The apprenticeship system must be revived if art is not to die. The secret is in doing one's work with "the affection that attention engenders" (130). He proposes that sketching clubs be formed for people who really want to draw. "The secrets of success," Butler adds, in a passage that tells us much about his own career, "are affection for the pursuit chosen, a flat refusal to be hurried or to pass anything as understood which is not understood, and an obstinacy of character which shall make the student's friends find it less trouble to let him have his own way than to bend him into theirs" (137).

A visit to the sanctuary at Oropa leads Butler to some direct speculations regarding the social order, something rare in his works. Here at Oropa a free vacation in the mountains under clean and attractive conditions is offered to the peasantry, much as books and art are offered free in the libraries and galleries of London. Since sleep and a glimpse of comfort are more important to the workingman than books and art, Butler suggests that recreation centers be established in England. He proposes as a start that Oxford and Cambridge be turned into such centers, making them "universities in deed as well as in name" (164–65).

Butler regards "the 'earnestness,' and 'intenseness,' and 'aestheticism,' and 'culture' (for they are in the end one) of the present day" as "so many attempts to conceal weakness" (170). He wishes that moderns could combine the "religious fervour" of Milton and Handel with these artists' ability to appreciate the virtues of paganism. But, he says, this "seems to have become impossible to Protestants since the time of Dr. Arnold" (169). He is convinced that those religions and cultures that are sure of an absolute and eternal standard are so on the surface only. More insight reveals that "nothing is absolutely important or absolutely unimportant, absolutely good or absolutely bad" (174). "We Protestants do not understand, nor take any very great pains to understand, the Church of Rome. If we did, we should find it to be in many respects as much in advance of us as it is behind us in others" (247).

At the religious festival at Locarno, Butler is amused by large American advertisements of a man in a black felt hat smoking a cigarette. "During the illuminations the unwonted light threw its glare upon the effigies of saints and angels, but it illumined also the man in the black felt hat" (248). When the celebrants fell asleep that night on the pavement and under the arches, "the busy persistent vibrations that rise in Anglo-Saxon brains were radiating from every wall, and the man in the black felt hat . . . [was] lying in wait, as a cat over a mouse's hole, to insinuate [himself] into the hearts of the people as soon as they should wake" (248). A prophetic picture for 1881!

Alps and Sanctuaries contains many passages of praise for relaxation and good sense: for pilgrims enjoying their pilgrimages, church dignitaries with a sense of humor; for the grace of a life led above the curse of conventionality and affectation. In a sense it is Butler's realization projected onto the face of his beloved Italy of the world that might have been had he been freed from the religious oppressiveness of his youth and from the narrow puritanism of the Victorian world. Unlike *The Way of All Flesh* on which he was then at work, it is free of anger and resentment; its occasional excursions into satire and criticism are good-humored, and all in all it is the most endearing and winning of Butler's expositions of his philosophy of life. In a way it fills out the incomplete picture at the end of his famous novel of the reality Ernest Pontifex can be seen moving toward after his sufferings and tribulations. It is easy to understand why some admirers of Butler's work regard this relaxed and friendly volume as his very best.

Chapter Five
The Way of All Flesh

In 1873, undaunted by the financial failure of *The Fair Haven,* Butler began work on a novel that was to become *The Way of All Flesh.* On 16 August he sent the first fifteen pages to Miss Savage. She was delighted with it. " 'Never have I been so calm, so soothed, so happy, so filled with a blessed peace' etc. as this morning when the first installment of your novel came," she wrote. "If it goes on as it begins, it will be a perfect novel or as nearly so as may be."[1] On 3 September she reported to Butler that she liked the second chapter even better than the first;[2] on 9 September she commented on chapter 5,[3] showing that the work was going ahead. Comments such as the following, scattered over the years, are the most fully participating ones that Butler received from anyone concerning his work:[4] "When am I to have more MS?"[5] (30 August 1873); "All that I have read is delightful,"[6] (20 July 1883); "The grand catastrophe wants vraisemblance.—Your Towneley, too, must be toned down—a coarse creature with vicious propensities. . . . Ernest gets tant soit peu priggish—in fact very much so—towards the end, and especially in the treatment of his children." (17 November 1883); "I think it is almost perfect this time."[7] (2 December 1883). Miss Savage projected herself into the novel and lived in it as Butler wrote it. It is not too much to say that he kept at it because of her delighted response.

At first Butler could not make up his mind about the narrative method he had adopted—using an observer, Overton, to tell his story. He rewrote some of the early material, dispensing with this observer. Then Miss Savage stated her preference for the story as told by a narrator; she said: "I prefer an advocate of flesh and blood," and pointed out that the use of a storyteller would allow naturally for interpretive comment.[8] Since the presence of Overton permits Butler to be ironic even about his most cherished ideas, we can be grateful that Miss Savage felt that way.[9] On 24 November she discussed Butler's portrait of Alethea with him, though it does not appear that she ever knew that he was drawing a picture of her.[10]

But late in 1873 Butler's financial troubles took his attention away from his novel, and then his work on *Life and Habit* absorbed him. Not until 1878 did he resume work on *The Way of All Flesh*. By 27 June, he had progressed to chapter 41, and he hoped to have the novel completed by April 1879. In 1879, however, he was still busy rewriting parts of it. He worked on the novel again in 1883, and finally set it aside because he realized that he could not publish it while his father and sisters were alive. He was also in genuine doubt as to its value.[11] Jones tells us that after Miss Savage's death in 1885 Butler did nothing more to the manuscript. It was, Jones is convinced, too closely associated with her in his mind, and he felt a sense of guilt for what he regarded as his egotistical behavior toward her.[12]

Daniel F. Howard links Butler's sporadic work on the novel with the rise and fall of his hatred for his father and surmises that he never revised the final sections of the novel or published the book because by 1884 he had become "a settled, self-justified man."[13] This unkind view of the older Butler accords poorly with the outpouring of literary work that went on for the rest of his life. It may be that Butler stopped work on *The Way of All Flesh* not because he associated the book with Miss Savage or thought he could not publish it, or because he had become "settled" and "self-justified," and needed hatred to keep him going, but because he was embarking on a complex task: tracing the near destruction of a young man by the stupidity of his parents, the achievement of a new type of human fulfillment not related to traditional norms of success (a happy marriage, a family, recognition, social position), and over all the demonstration of the workings of the instinctive and inherited evolutionary forces described in his *Life and Habit* theory. After all, he was doing something quite strange and original in creating what we would now call an "existential" hero, in his passivity not unlike Camus's Stranger. Presiding over all this like the Greek goddess Athena over the fate of Telemachus is the spirit of Alethea (the truth) who in this sense is the spirit of Miss Savage.

The Generations of Men

The Way of All Flesh covers five generations though concentrating on the fourth and allows Butler by his creation of a genial but stuffy observer Overton from the third generation to provide theory and interpretation again and again, giving the book a solid grounding in theorizing about evolution and unconscious memory. The novel begins with the hero's great-grandfather, John Pontifex, a village carpenter, embodying in his existence the sweetness of the old English rural way of life and a worshipper of the sun—he "had two steps built up against a wall in the kitchen garden on which he used to stand and watch the sun go down whenever it was clear" and just before his death he said "Good bye sun, good bye sun" (13). Avrom Fleishman calls this the first hint that something unconventional and quite outside the usual bounds of Victorian fiction (he calls it "strange") is being said in this novel, and reminds us that Ernest also sees a vision in the sun (170–71). "The subtler implication is that Ernest can look far back in his ancestry and find progenitors who have *not* travelled down the road of the Pontifexes . . . that there is an essential self or zoosperm at the outset of the individual's career that is somehow recoverable."[14]

Old John Pontifex paints, plays an organ he himself built, and, according to a passage Butler wrote but deleted, had himself once seen Handel, whom he regarded as the greatest of all musicians (4). He also shows by his effective but kindly disciplining of his own boy that unlike his son and grandson after him he knows how a parent should scold a child (5). Overton's father says of John "He was one of the very ablest men I ever knew." (6). In a way this old carpenter is the hero of the novel in that he represents not just an attractive exterior of "good breeding" as Towneley does, but an interior ideal of a human being who is talented in many fields, unselfconscious, unegotistic, modest, considerate of others, and in short an unacclaimed genius in whatever he does. He thus quietly achieves the goal of Ernest's own thwarted strivings. He is in this sense the embodiment of Butler's speculations in his NoteBooks, in *Life and Habit,* and indeed throughout his work on what it means to be human: in his simple way, he represents, as Handel does on a grand scale, the achievement of unconscious perfection.

Old Pontifex has a domineering wife who has no sense of humor and may be seen as the biological "cross" that brings ambition, self-consciousness, domineering, the drive for worldly success, into the line. Perhaps as a direct result of this infusion George Pontifex, their only child, becomes highly successful in the worldly sense. Ironically, he makes his money as a publisher of religious books. Historically, his rise represents the new commercial standards of his day, as opposed to the old rural ones. Overton's father, with Butlerian insight, refuses to praise George for his worldly success, and says that one John Pontifex is worth one hundred George Pontifexes (7). One critic even regards George as the villain of the novel.[15] Certainly it is his tyrannical treatment of his son Theobald that sets the pattern for Theobald's treatment of Ernest that so nearly destroys him.

Overton, the narrator, sees some of this, but not all. Perhaps, he speculates, George had risen too rapidly in life to be sure of himself; perhaps he was a throwback to a previous ancestor, or was more like his mother than his father. In any case, taken all in all, he was a successful man: "Having lived to be nearly seventy-three years old and died rich he must have been in very fair harmony with his surroundings. . . . The psalmist says, "The righteous shall not lack anything that is good.' Either this is mere poetical licence, or it follows that he who lacks anything that is good is not righteous. . . . [George] Pontifex never lacked anything he much cared about" (73). All of this is highly satirical of conventional pieties in typical Butlerian fashion.

George is certainly not the man his father was. He shows no compunction about lying in the presence of Gelstrap, his servant, who knows he is lying. Worst of all, he is a master at torturing his children under the impression that he is doing them good. Yet again the complacent Overton observes, "It shows no great moral obliquity on the part of parents if within certain limits they make their children's lives a burden to them" (74). The evil in this novel certainly comes from those whom Overton understands and to an extent even forgives, who tolerate and encourage will-shaking, useless educations, browbeating of children, and from men who do not know the art of being themselves.

More space and detail are devoted to the portrait of Theobald, George's son and the chief victim of his aggressiveness and cruelty. His story represents the third stage in the fivefold novel. Theobald has cause to revolt, but he unconsciously, in Butler's theory and in conformity with accepted patterns, chooses the path of revenge, doing unto his children as had been done unto him—only more so. A glimmer of resistance flickers when he audaciously proposes to his father that he not enter the ministry. But George subdues him with one blow: " 'You shall not receive a single six-pence from me till you come to your senses' " (33). Theobald surrenders.

Butler has been accused of caricaturing his own father in the portrait of Theobald. Significantly, he wrote to his sister May on 12 November 1873, after he had begun the book, that he had written no work drawing on any living person, and would never do so.[16] Obviously, however, Theobald's abortive revolt and Ernest's real one are both patterned on Butler's own. And so many other details of the Theobald Pontifex family life are drawn directly from Butler's youth, including the letter taken verbatim from one his mother wrote for him and his brother,[17] that no one can deny that the novel has much basis in reality. The point, though, is that the artistic duplication of events, the arrangement, and the meaning are poetic creations and not slavish transcripts. It is surely a mistake, as Arnold Silver points out,[18] to regard Ernest as merely a portrait of the author, or Theobald as merely a portrait of the author's father.

The story of Theobald is told briefly, succinctly, acidly. We should remember if we are repelled by it that in many respects it is the same as the story of Ernest which, beginning with chapter 20, will be told in fuller detail and with greater warmth. Neither story is complete without the other. In the second telling there is more sympathy and understanding, more of the complex vision of many points of view; and the whole is much closer to what we expect of a novel. Theobald does his best in bringing up his son to adhere to the evangelical standards of his day, and it is only from the standpoint of a double vision that we may see him as cruel, dishonest, and cowardly. With the exception of Overton, Theobald's children, the butler John, Mrs. Jupp, Alethea, and perhaps the reader of the novel, everyone regards Theobald as a perfect man, underlining the fact that he is doing what the world expects: "He was beloved by all who had anything to do with him." And Overton adds, "The general verdict is often the truest" (350). Here again Butler's narrator by his moralizing subverts the meaning of the novel's events; most readers cannot forgive Theobald for his overbearing egotistical cruelty to his son and indeed cannot even believe that Overton could forgive him. Ralf Norrman in his stylistic-based analysis of Butler in passages like this suggests that Butler's deep-seated dualism prevented him from ever allowing one side of an argument to win out, so that after really demolishing Theobald by the events of the story he must have Overton rise to his defense;[19] but can any sensitive reader of *The Way of All Flesh* believe that Theobald was a lovable man?

Butler, Claude T. Bissell pointed out, is developing in *The Way of All Flesh* "the conception of personality, the theory of the unconscious, the emphasis on life as a manifestation of shaping will, the biological approach to problems of human conduct . . . that have passed into the main current of modern thought,"[20]—and all of this development can be seen as we follow the generations of Pontifexes through Overton's watchful but too complacent eyes. Again, there is "a covert religion at work in the text," according to Fleishman, which is implied in the book's generalized title,[21] and this religion is Butler's image of humanity and his theory of unconscious albeit purposive evolution.

A New Interpretation of Life

Aside from the originality and modernity of *The Way of All Flesh* as seen by Bissell and the "covert religion" that Fleishman finds, and perhaps also because of them, the novel is in many respects a high point of the attempt to look at life from an unaccustomed angle, as is also so much else in Butler: it is not merely satire or irony, but an interpretation of the nature of existence, and an interpretation that those unaccustomed to upside-down thinking find bitter, cold, uncaring. For example, hidden beneath the surface of every marriage, under the publicly accepted features, is the obverse side of exploitation, fear, mistrust, and shock, even though sentimental people refuse to admit this. To have a wedding described in terms of these hidden features appalls those who accept the public facade as the only reality. Mr. Heatherley's reactions are typical. Butler tells us that he "said I had taken all the tenderest feelings of our nature and, having spread them carefully over the floor, stamped upon them till I had reduced them to an indistinguishable mass of filth . . . I do not take this view of the matter myself."[22] Like Butler, we too must not take this view.

Since if it does not repel us, the unexpected makes us laugh, the account of Theobald's courtship of Christina and of their marriage strikes readers as uproariously funny. Butler indeed wanted it to do so. Like all real humor, however, it is tragic as well as funny—and sometimes we do not know whether to laugh or weep at this surprisingly inverse but convincing world to which we are introduced. A letter proposing marriage is generally a touching thing, but Overton concludes his transcript of Theobald's letter to Christina with the comment: "And this was all that his public school and University education had been able to do for Theobald!" (43).

Theobald's father, on hearing of his son's engagement, might have been portrayed as an injured parent for whom we should feel sorry. Instead, the narrator comments that the occasion "afforded a golden opportunity which the old gentleman . . . embraced with characteristic eagerness" (49). What a shock to learn that vindictiveness is something we enjoy! Hardly a page of the novel presents events in their ordinary light. Rather than bitterness, what is operating in it is a greater perceptiveness than we are accustomed to. Sigmund Freud was not the first to see that men's real motives are often quite different from what they think they are.

The subversive view of Victorian morality, and indeed of all morality too, which pervades the entire novel, whereby the traditionally virtuous becomes evil and the evil virtuous, comes before us in passage after passage and event after event and is the most striking feature of the book. One critic speculates that Butler is defending the view of life of the English lower classes and of the highest aristocracy in opposition to middle-class morality, and thus is initiating a new trend in the novel which led directly to D. H. Lawrence's later works.[23] There is truth in this view, but in a sense it is coincidental. Butler wrote this way not through a sentimental attachment for the underdog but because he was deeply convinced that, in the light of what Victorian morality and all puritanical morality was doing to people, the happiness of mankind demanded a "transvaluation of all values," to use a phrase invented by Nietzsche. His notebooks show repeatedly, as does *The Way of All Flesh,* that he celebrated the greater openness of the pagan world over the puritanical introspection and righteousness of Christianity, and to clinch this conviction was sure that Handel in the joyousness of his pagan rituals did so too (for example, the Dagon chorus in *Samson*).

Mr. Allaby, a rector with nine children and an income of £600 a year, would normally be admired by the middle class for his spiritual, self-sacrificing life. Overton comments about anyone who could get himself into such a predicament: "If morality is that which, on the whole, brings a man peace in his declining years—if, that is to say, it is not an utter swindle—can you under these circumstances flatter yourself that you have led a moral life? . . . Someone should do for morals what that old Pecksniff Bacon has obtained the credit of having done for science" (34–35).

Traditionally, we admire a parent who has his children well educated. Overton observes about George Pontifex who tried to accomplish this result: "He did not see that the education cost the children far more than it cost him, inasmuch as it cost them the power of earning their living easily . . . and ensured their being at the mercy of their father for years" (23). He finds the church catechism wanting: "I should like to introduce a few words insisting on the duty of seeking all reasonable pleasure and avoiding all pain that can be honourably avoided" (30). And the scorching light thrown upon the harmful effects of a silly religiosity in the aspirations of Christina, bordering as they do on mania, is excruciating: the knife of the skillful surgeon is at work here, cutting away what desperately needs to be removed. " 'We, dearest Theobald,' " she exclaims to her fiancé, " 'will be ever faithful. We will stand firm and support one another even in the hour of death itself. God in his mercy may spare us from being burnt alive. . . . O Lord . . . spare my Theobald, or grant that he may be beheaded.' " Whereupon Theobald replies: " 'Such a life let us pray God that it may please Him to enable us to pray that we may lead.' " "The moon had risen," Overton concludes this episode, "and the arbour was getting damp, so they adjourned further aspirations for a more convenient season" (48).

Immediately after his marriage Theobald's real self protests the trap that deference to tradition has sprung upon him. For Butler, this self is the being within Theobald made up of his ancestral memories and is a much safer guide than his fallible and foolish conscious self. "He didn't mean to have married Christina [Overton tells us]: he hadn't married her; it was all a hideous dream; he would—But a voice kept ringing in his ears which said: 'YOU CAN'T, CAN'T, CAN'T.' 'CAN'T I?' screamed the unhappy creature to himself. 'NO,' said the remorseless voice, 'YOU CAN'T. YOU ARE A MARRIED MAN' " (52).

The complex humor of *The Way of All Flesh* resides, as Fleishman points out,[24] in Butler's ability to reduce usually sacrosanct items like courtship and marriage "to materials of play" (though a bitter kind of play!) and pompously to restate the enemy's position, as often happens in Overton's moralizing, or to use the enemy's voice. "You are surrounded on every side by lies," Ernest's real self says to him, talking exactly like the Old Testament God, "which would deceive even the elect, if the elect were not generally so uncommonly wide awake; the self of which you are conscious, your reasoning and reflecting self, will believe these lies and bid you act in accordance with them. This conscious self of yours, Ernest, is a prig begotten of prigs and trained in priggishness; I will not allow it to shape your actions. . . . Obey *me,* your true self, and things will go tolerably well with you, but only listen to that outward and visible husk of yours which is called your father, and I will rend you in pieces even unto the third and fourth generation as one who has hated God; for I, Ernest, am the God who made you' " (161).

Margaret Ganz believes that Butler's ironic transposings of values in *The Way of All Flesh* provides a diagnosis of reality by presenting the "uncertainty and contradiction at the heart of experience." She argues persuasively that by his use of irony Butler "disengage[s] the self from surface conventions" and the loss this entails "plays a strategic role in achieving wholeness'';[25] the stripping away accomplished by irony leads to the retrieving of the crucial hidden life or real self that Butler was among the first to discover. Butler, she argues, is a "true precursor of Freud" and *The Way of All Flesh* is "a case history in the development of the ego."[26]

In drawing the portrait of Christina, Butler makes use of a device he had begun to use in *The Fair Haven* to present the daydreams of John Pickard Owen's mother. It is a forerunner of the stream-of-consciousness technique used by later novelists, so many of whom were influenced by *The Way of All Flesh*. "For Ernest a very great future— she was certain of it—was in store. . . . Heaven would bear her witness that she had never shrunk from the idea of martyrdom for herself and Theobald, nor would she avoid it for her boy, if his life was required of her in her Redeemer's service. Oh, no! . . . It was not for nothing that Ernest had been baptized in water from the Jordan. . . . Why, it was a miracle! It was! It was! She saw it all now. The Jordan had left its bank and flowed into her own house. . . . And so on for hours together day after day for years" (89–91). These daydreams occur again and again in the novel, culminating in a final glorious one as Christina is dying and sees Ernest in Parliament, made Prime Minister, raised to the peerage as Lord Battersby, and herself immortalized in a famous "Portrait of Lord Battersby's Mother,"—"and so on till her daughter told her it was time to take her medicine" (325). Christina, one critic thinks,[27] in spite of her weakness and cruelty to her son, represents the heart of the novel: she is incapable of her husband's coldness, and although she lives in a fantasy world, her longings are full of generosity and love. But this view is hard to accept when one remembers her silly daydreams and her treacherous betrayal of Ernest time after time.

The Wayward Hero

Ernest, Theobald's and Christina's son, the fourth generation, and the novel's central character, arouses our compassion. True, he is passive, and much of his life is a "failure" in any worldly sense, but we are made to see so clearly the power of the forces allied against him in the coerciveness of his parents, the dulling effect of his drilling in the classical languages, the total failure of anyone except his aunt Alethea to encourage him to develop as his own organism wants to, that we would be hard-hearted indeed if we were not moved by his plight.

We are told that when he was two his father began to teach him to read, and began to whip him two days after he had begun to teach him (81). Then Overton, recounting a visit to the Pontifex household shortly thereafter, describes Theobald's dragging Ernest off to the diningroom for a beating when he said "tum" instead of "come." " 'I have sent him up to bed,' said Theobald, as he returned to the drawingroom, 'and now, Christina, I think we will have the servants in to prayers,' and he rang the bell for them, red-handed as he was" (86). This "red-handed" suggests real murder.[28]

We are touched by Ernest's desire to love all things that will allow him to do so. "It was long," Overton tells us, before his mother "could destroy all affection for herself in the mind of her first-born. But she persevered." (79). Our compassion for Ernest, however, does not make us see him as a conventional hero. He is clearly a precursor of the twentieth-century antihero, even the existentialist hero. For most of the novel he is passive, reacting to blows dealt out to him, but initiating little. Even his aunt Alethea's help is dissipated by her untimely death. She knows that her godson can be strengthened if he is allowed to "kiss the soil" (254), as Butler was in New Zealand. She arranges for him to have carpentry lessons, and, knowing his love for Handel, asks him to build an organ for her. When she unexpectedly dies she leaves her estate to come to Ernest at age twenty-eight, but Ernest does not know this. All this understanding and affection have no abiding effect: when Alethea dies, Theobald immediately stops the organ building (note the suggestion of a frustration of the arrival at sexual maturity) and the carpentry lessons. Ernest's continuing love of music appears merely as a futile decoration in his apparently rudderless life.

On the few occasions when Ernest does compulsively take charge of events he makes nothing but errors: because he has never been allowed to practice taking the initiative, like a startled snipe he darts off unpredictably. At Cambridge, preparing for holy orders, he is swept off his feet by an evangelist and shocks his family by a sudden conversion to a religious fervor abhorrent to their smug Anglicanism; he is hoodwinked by a high-church scoundrel who talks him into a harebrained scheme to set up a "College of Spiritual Pathology"; and he engages in other erratic escapades, one of which lands him in prison. Even Overton loses faith in him.

The climax and turning point comes with his arrest and with his decision to break with his past. These are artfully led up to by his encounter with the free thinker Mr. Shaw, who in a few words shows

Ernest that he knows nothing about the Bible, by his hearing Towneley, his hero, say " 'No, no, no' " (254) to his whole way of life, and by his reading the *Vestiges of Creation,* that book which on its publication in 1844 raised a storm of protest by its use of geological evidence to cast doubt on the biblical story of creation. On his discharge, Theobald and Christina are at the prison gate to receive him. " 'We must never leave him to himself' " Theobald says, and Christina adds, " 'Our voices [will be] the first to exhort him to return to the paths of virtue' " (262).

Ernest was as white as a sheet. His heart beat so that he could hardly breathe. . . . Then, gathering strength, he said . . . 'Mother, . . . we must part.' . . . Theobald stepped forward. 'Ernest, you must not, shall not, leave us in this way.' 'Do not speak to me' said Ernest, his eyes flashing with a fire that was unwonted in them. . . . 'Tell them [he said to the Warden] from me that they must think of me as one dead, for I am dead to them.' . . . After he had got a few steps out he turned his face to the prison wall, leant against it for support, and wept as though his heart would break. (263).

Strengthened by his prison term and his discovery that he can be his own man, Ernest has thus at last begun to hear the voice within him. This voice will express his unconscious memories and lead him slowly, after additional blunders and suffering, as he learns to hear it, to become himself. It is one of Butler's "modern" insights, repeated by many a later writer, that the break with parents is the beginning of self-realization. Butler has added a new dimension to the time-honored tradition of the bildungsroman.

What It Means

The resolution of the novel has often been criticized.[29] Butler never revised the last part as he had intended to, and it is therefore long and discursive: it needs tightening. But the central theme is unmistakable. Ernest wishes to become a philosophical writer who by his writings will help mankind to better itself, to avoid the mistakes he has made. Significantly, his first big project is to gather information about the marriage customs of many races, to ascertain which people are the happiest, and to report his findings to his countrymen. This does not mean that he has become another Samuel Butler or another Overton or that his career peters out into futility and pettiness. The great Victorian literary tradition held that the writer is a cultural leader. Butler was scornful of men such as Carlyle and Arnold because he rejected their premises, but he was not scornful of literature as a dialogue carried on with vigor, honesty, and skill. Our contemporary conviction that the artist—whether he be novelist, poet, or dramatist—can be more effective than the philosophical writer, essayist, or even journalist, is not necessarily the right one.[30] Ernest is no more futile in his dedication than Stephan Dedalus is in his. In his vision of the future, *Das Glasperlenspiel (Magister Ludi)*, Hermann Hesse sees our period as one of journalism. Why should not men like Ernest contribute to the future creatively, as Butler tried to do?

John B. Rosenman maintains that *The Way of All Flesh* is the most significant Victorian document dealing with Evangelicalism and suggests that in it Butler seeks to get at the "spirit" or "main idea" of his religious upbringing rather than to reject it altogehter.[31] Naseeb Shaheen actually finds that there are 490 biblical references in the novel, outnumbering all other references, whether classical, musical, scientific, or from art, and that these range from a sarcastic undercutting use to a direct use of traditional meanings, to symbolic reinterpretations to fit Butler's own worldview.[32] These thoughtful studies, however, seem to overlook the larger thrust of the novel, apart from Overton's more complacent insights, of real outrage over what Christian religiosity has done to human beings.

The Way of All Flesh can be seen, as Fleishman sees it, as "standing among the most artful of autobiographical novels" and also as the author's way "of objectifying the being that he struggled to make of himself against such odds." Butler "reduces both his immature and his mature selves to aesthetic objects and directs the same ironic light on each."[33] Surely, though, Butler the writer is a more powerful figure than Ernest the character ever could become. It may be that Butler wished Ernest different from what he actually is. A subtle clue to this possibility can be found in the use of musical metaphor throughout the novel.[34] All the positive characters are identified in one way or another with the music of Handel, yet Ernest himself cannot stay in the key of C but always modulates into C sharp (353). But if Butler was finally disappointed with both Ernest and Overton, he does not say so except by the calmness of the novel's peroration. There are no shouts of bravo, no heroic posings at the novel's end. If there is victory, it is internal. Ernest, however flawed, has become his own man, a builder of bridges (one of the meanings of *Pontifex*) into an uncertain and nebulous future.

Certainly *The Way of All Flesh* is far from the traditional novel, sure to please a wide audience of Butler's and Miss Savage's day, and the hope of founding a literary career on it and earning money that was in both their minds at the start[35] could hardly have been fulfilled for many years. Whence came this surprising innovation in novel writing? Like each of Butler's books, *The Way of All Flesh* came from within, and it is a testimony to Miss Savage's open-mindedness that she did not point out to the author how unlikely his fiction was to succeed at once. Perhaps she saw what Margaret Ganz sees, that this novel, like Ernest's one successful book, rings "with the courage alike of conviction and of an entire absence of conviction."[36] "Butler's approach," she writes, "mutes even as it illumines the pain of the genetic bind and more largely affirms the existential imperative of the ironist—the command that he live sanely and die well by unearthing the truths our mortal unease has attempted to bury."[37] She sees Butler as a man on a perilous balloon journey, uncertain "what to save and what to jettison," and using irony to help him decide, even though irony cannot set him free because "it always remembers reality."[38] In this sense, *The Way of All Flesh* becomes an image of Butler's life. Ernest has indeed finally come to himself.

Chapter Six
Widening Circles

With the manuscript of his most important work unpublished,[1] Butler turned to a variety of other projects in his continuing attempt to speak to his era. These included, as we have seen, his books on evolution.

The "Earnest Clergyman"

During the spring of 1879 he published under various pseudonyms a series of letters in the *Examiner*. In them he carefully developed several conflicting points of view about the dilemma of a clergyman who is supposed, after having studied *Essays and Reviews*, Bishop Colenso, and Darwin,[2] to have become a skeptic. This "Earnest Clergyman" writes the first two letters. He is middle-aged, married, has five children, and has no way of earning a living if he leaves his post. What is he to do?

"Cantab." writes the third letter in the series. He points out that no one should be blamed for not being heroic, since heroism is exceptional behavior. He therefore urges the "Earnest Clergyman" to stick to his post, saying that even though the "Clergyman" rejects some church doctrines, he can work on the practical, moral level and make a worthy contribution to the cause of a better life. To this the "Clergyman" replies that he wants to be neither too far ahead nor too far behind the average man, but he cannot base his life upon a fiction. A third letter writer, "Oxoniensis," now appears who attacks the "cultured scepticism" of "Cantab." and states categorically that Christianity, being divine, is either all true in every detail or nothing but a fraud. No self-respecting man, he argues, can remain a minister unless he believes wholly and absolutely in the doctrine of his church. A fourth debater, "Ethics," thereupon states his conviction that it is better to deceive others knowing that we are doing so, as the "Earnest Clergyman" is doing, than to deceive ourselves as "Cantab." has urged. He gives examples of animals and plants that make their living by deception, and he says that the individual man cannot settle the great questions of his life for himself, but must do what he is called upon to do.

"Cantab." defends himself by drawing a distinction between the divine truth, which must be perfect, and the limited truth, which is all that man knows. On the basis of this latter truth man can work in the practical sphere, even if he rejects some of it. "Oxoniensis" immediately attacks this distinction, calling it unmanly and fraudulent; but "Cantab." replies that it is irrational to say that Christianity is either all right or all wrong. The question to be raised is: What can *we* know to be true?

After "Ethics" writes to agree with "Cantab.," a fifth writer, "Lewis Wright," points out that all men must lie to some extent. What is the fisherman but a liar when he disguises his hook with a worm? The thirteenth contribution to the series is Butler's poem "The Righteous Man," signed "X.Y.Z." In this poem he holds up to scorn those who do good only when force is on their side. Then the "Earnest Clergyman" rejects the views of both "Cantab." and "Oxoniensis" as too extreme; he argues that the crucial requirement in all such matters is to avoid the shock that comes from pushing too fast and too far.

The exchange concludes with two letters from other clergymen both of whom describe themselves as caught in the dilemma of the "Earnest Clergyman" and who warn young men thinking of the ministry to take heed before it is too late. "E.D." says, "I wish to save some from the mental torture which I have endured" (*Collected Essays,* 1, 98), and "Sollicitus" adds, "Earnestly would I join with 'E.D.' in exhorting young men thinking of orders to pause, or they may find themselves in evil case in after years" (99).

These letters suggest that Butler was still wrestling with his decision against becoming a clergyman and wondering what would have happened to him had he given in to his father's wishes, entered the ministry, settled down, and raised a family. The letters dramatize the problem without giving anyone a clear victory. Since Butler now felt a growing conviction that the spirit of religion was right, but not the letter, it is obvious that he could wonder whether he had been right to give in to his youthful skepticism: perhaps he could have served the cause of the "true" religion based on his *Life and Habit* theory from within the church. There are those who think Butler at his best when he examines opposing views as here rather than when he champions one solution, as in his books on evolution and his later Homeric, Shakespearean, and art studies.[3] This, however, is to deny to Butler a large segment of his life and to rule arbitrarily that we must know by some divine canon what would have been better for him than what he himself did and desired. Butler himself recognized the danger of dogmatism: on 2 August 1874 he had written to Miss Savage: "I will not be didactic—at least I will watch and pray that I may not be so; but being didactic is a sin that doth most easily beset me."[4] Yet the fact remains that he was really not sorry he had chosen as he had. As late as 1887 he wrote to a friend: "Till Christianity is dead and buried we shall never get the burning questions that lie beyond approached in a spirit of sobriety and commonsense. It is therefore against superstition, and more especially the Christian superstition, that I have fought to the best of my ability."[5]

"God the Known and God the Unknown"

Following this exchange of letters, the *Examiner* in May, June, and July of 1879 published a series of articles that Butler called "God the Known and God the Unknown." In these he attempts to become definite about the possible theological implications of his *Life and Habit* theory. The articles do less than justice to the subtlety of his mind, however, and lack the suggestive and imaginative power of his books of this period. Although passages in the *Note-Books* develop the ideas here set forth, it is hard to believe that Butler is as sure of himself as he pretends to be.

Briefly put, Butler's argument goes as follows. Given the identity of all life to which his theory of memory led, each living being can be thought of as a part of the known God. We ourselves thus are God, and He exists and expresses Himself through us. This known God can arouse real emotion. Butler writes:

The theologian dreams of a God sitting above the clouds among the cherubim, who blow their loud uplifted angel trumpets before Him, and humor Him as though He were some despot in an Oriental tale; but we enthrone Him upon the wings of birds, on the petals of flowers, on the faces of our friends, and upon whatever we most delight in of all that lives upon the earth. We then can not only love Him, but we can do that without which love has neither power nor sweetness, but is a phantom only, an impersonal person, a vain stretching forth of arms towards something that can never fill them— we can express our love and have it expressed to us in return. And this not in the uprearing of stone temples—for the Lord dwelleth in temples made with other organs than hands—nor yet in the cleansing of our hearts, but in the caress bestowed upon horse and dog, and kisses upon the lips of those we love. (*Collected Essays*, 1, 37–38)

This is eloquent and moving. But to explain the origin of this known God in whom we participate, Butler goes on to say that we may imagine a greater unknown God of whom the known God is a part as each cell is a part of us. This transcendent God at which he thus arrives seems distant, unreal, and little better than the gods of the pantheist or the anthropomorphist which he rejects. The argument bogs down in the materialistic cause-and-effect thinking of his era that Butler, at his best, rose above. The unknown God is simply not capable of bearing the emotional and theological weight he attempts to put upon Him. Emerson and Thoreau might have understood and sympathized with his known God; they would have rejected the matter-of-fact reasoning leading to the unknown God. Significantly, Butler never republished these articles, and he never again tried to set forth so definite a theology.

Whistling in the Dark

In 1886, as we have seen, Canon Butler died and Butler's financial problems were finally resolved. He now had more than enough money to meet his needs. He "bought a pair of new hair brushes and a larger wash-hand basin";[6] he soon hired Alfred Emery Cathie to be his clerk, valet, and secretary; and he allowed Henry Festing Jones a stipend to enable him to spend more time working with him. A subtle change took place in Butler as he grew older and more secure. With his best work either unpublished or, when published, vilified (even though a few words of praise were heard from time to time), he had won no real audience and had been operating pretty much in a vacuum. His tendency toward elaborate pretense of scorn for the opinion of others, his strong conviction that an artist must do what he wants to do no matter what people say, had slowly become a mode of whistling in the dark. There is no doubt that he gradually adopted a kind of bravado to shield himself from the subtle corrections that, as he well knew, reality forces upon the healthy organism. No elaborate inner explanation needs to be sought for the maladjustment that grew more noticeable in him from this time on—the slightly ridiculous world of good fellowship he built up with Jones, Cathie, and a small circle of friends; the somewhat exaggerated fussiness about his various theories; and the odd causes he championed. The explanation is at hand in the absence of a proper "loading factor" in the form of a critical and appreciative audience for what he did.

All this is not to say that the work of Butler's concluding period was negligible. Even in these final sixteen years his writing remains interesting and provocative, and he continues to evince a remarkable measure of sanity and imagination. But his conviction that the polite, cultured self-satisfaction of the established groups of his day, especially of the scientists and scholars, was a monumental sham became sharper and sharper as the years passed, right up to the end of his life. As time went on, he was to make things harder for the few of his contemporaries who attended to him and for those of us who read him now. It is as though he were taking revenge for his lonely position and crying out, "Just see if you can agree with me!"

Ex Voto

Butler, of course, had always been interested in art, an interest illustrated most notably by his unsuccessful attempt to become a professional painter. In 1886 he had applied for the Slade Professorship of Art at Cambridge, which was, however, given to C. H. Middleton. In his notebooks and in his other books, especially in *Alps and Sanctuaries,* he repeatedly reformulated his conviction that conventional academic art was the death of the true artistic impulse, and like others of his time—the Pre-Raphaelites, for example—he sought a return to more primitive, more natural expression. In addition to all this came his abiding longing for a striking discovery, his repeated conviction that he had made one, followed by his repeated disillusionment because no one would admit that he had. The really amazing fact in all this is his stubborn insistence on forging onwards to ever newer and more improbable discoveries when most men would have given up. His demure politeness and graciousness described by those who knew him[7] were a facade protecting a man who had real steel in his soul.

When Butler wrote *Alps and Sanctuaries,* he did not discuss Varallo-Sesia, in his opinion the most important of the north Italian sanctuaries, because, as he stated, it deserved a book to itself. He now wrote that book—*Ex Voto,* published in 1888. It is a detailed analysis, appraisal, and study of the various groups of statues in the forty-five chapels on the sacred mountain at Varallo, each chapel presenting a key event from the Bible and from the life of the Saviour. Work on the site was begun at the end of the fifteenth century when a number of Franciscan brothers came to reside there, and continued on through the seventeenth century. Each chapel contains a complete scene to be viewed through the chapel's open side, showing wood, terra cotta, or stucco figures realistically painted and robed, grouped against a frescoed background. Sometimes there are as many as forty figures and, in one dramatization, nine horses too, all life-size. The view that Jones gives us of what Butler was doing is discouraging. Writing about Butler to Butler's artist friend, Charles Gogin, from Varallo which he and Butler were visiting, Jones says: "He has been making great progress with a new Italian book which is to run this place and Gaudenzio Ferrari. . . . There is another man who did statues up here, Tabachetti, who is also to be run."[8]

Butler had long felt that many learned men and scholars had built their reputations on the unscrupulous "running" of a theory, a more or less well-known figure, or a pet project in which he could hardly think that they believed. He was convinced that they were simply getting all the percentage they could from a special racket. Leaving aside the question of how consciously or unconsciously this was done, the idea makes a good satirical point about the ways of the learned world. The irony in this, however, is that apparently Butler is about to do the same thing he thought the professionals did. Does the "running" remain a game to him, in the spirit of Hesse's *Das Glasperlenspiel (Magister Ludi);* or is he, like the learned savants, to take it as his private racket? Jones's evaluation suggests cold-bloodedness. This can hardly have been the heart of the matter, but at least the phrasing of Jones's comment suggests that the idea probably came from Butler himself.[9]

All the paraphernalia of *Ex Voto* indicate complete seriousness on Butler's part—the endless hours of research in libraries and museums in preparing his book, the search for early sources, the careful documentation, the elaborate quarrels with experts in the field. Indeed, in this and in following works Butler revealed, as he had done in his books on evolution, the shortcomings, errors, and lack of scholarly care in those with whom he differed by bearing down with savage skill on specific points. His analysis in *Ex Voto* of Sir Henry Layard's discussion of Varallo is a good example (2–6); it stands comparison with Lessing's *Vademekum für Herrn Lange.* Yet, in general, the structure he proceeds to erect in the place of what he demolishes is not much more satisfactory than the demolished one; for he inevitably leaves many new loopholes open. It is an exciting and endless game, if game it really is.

The Sacri Monte at Varallo was neglected and run down; but, when Butler first visited it in 1871[10] and when he visited it again on many subsequent occasions, he was impressed by the beauty and naturalness of the biblical figures in the chapels. Perhaps they spoke to a hidden longing in him to have the world of traditional religion which he had rejected come to life in spite of himself. In any case, he became convinced that "Tabachetti's Journey to Calvary . . . is of such superlative excellence as regards composition and dramatic power, to say nothing of the many admirable individual figures comprised in it, that it is not too much to call it the most astounding work that has ever been achieved in sculpture" (62). Other complex forces working behind this "discovery" were Butler's instinctive sympathy for the outcast and unrecognized—derived from his awareness of his own position as an Ishmael—and his abiding desire to make discoveries in which no one else could claim a part.[11] An additional factor might be that "it drove its unhappy creator mad, which the Medicean chapel never did by Michael Angelo" (62).

Butler had bought two cameras, had taken some lessons in photography, and had spent many hours photographing the statues at Varallo. The pictures in his book do a good deal to help the reader understand his discussion, and they show also that he was not wrong to be enthusiastic about these figures. Caiaphas, for example, and St. Joseph are remarkable characterizations, masterfully executed. Il Vecchiotto, which he regarded as "perhaps the finest figure of all, who looks as if he had dropped straight from the heavens" (63), is not so impressive, unless one thinks of him as an embodiment of old John Pontifex.

One of Butler's primary aims in writing *Ex Voto* is again to persuade the reader to look upon art with his own eyes—not with the eyes of tradition. In his enthusiasm for the modest and unassuming he leans toward what in our time would be called a taste for the primitive. The opening chapters contain some excellent suggestions for acquiring a fresher, more spontaneous view of art. Butler likes Tabachetti more than Gaudenzio Ferrari because he had "a robustness, and freedom from mannerism and self-repetition, that are not always observable in Gaudenzio's work" (83). But there is a danger in his application of his own lesson. So enamored does he become of his insights that he convinces himself that every statue at Varallo and in the neighborhood which is unusually beautiful must be the work of Tabachetti, the master of them all; and he proceeds to build a castle of inferences upon his subjective preference. He draws, too, upon his own practices as a writer in assuming that striking portraits must be based on living beings and that he can detect resemblances to real people. Thus he finds three

portraits of Tabachetti himself, two of Leonardo da Vinci, and two of
Stefano Scotti.

Butler's view of greatness in art is linked with his conception of
unconscious perfection:

With few exceptions even the best art-work falls into one of two classes,
and offers signs either of immaturity or decline. . . . Michael Angelo said
the last word; but then he said just a word or two over. So with Titian
and Leonardo da Vinci, and in music with Haydn, Mozart, and Beethoven.
We . . . feel the presence of an autumnal tint over all the luxuriance of
development which . . . tells of an art that has taken not an upward but
a downward path. . . . It is only with the very few, as with Homer and
Shakespeare at their best . . . and in music with Handel, that I can see
no step left unclimbed, yet none taken on the downward path. (181)

Later, he speculates about the fickleness of fame: "We flatter ourselves
that among the kings and queens of art, music, and literature, or at
any rate in the kingdom of the great dead, all wrongs shall be redressed,
and patient merit shall take no more quips and scorns from the unworthy.
. . . It is not so. . . . The reputations of the great dead . . . are
governed in the main by the chicane that obtains among the living"
(201). Yet Butler recognizes that art must die: "How is it to end if
we go on at our present rate, with huge geological formations of art
and book middens accreting in every city of Europe? Who is to see
them, who even to catalogue them? . . . With such a surfeit of art
and science the mind palls and longs to be relieved from both. . . .
Let [a man's work] live in the use which passeth all praise or thanks
or even understanding, and let the story die after a certain time as all
things else must do" (203–4).

In concluding his work, Butler indulges in some generalizations about
the spirit of science and religion: "I, and those who think as I do,
would see the letter whether of science or of Christianity made less of,
and the spirit more. Slowly, but very slowly . . . things move in this
direction" (211). But "that the letter of the coming faith will be greatly
truer than that of the many that have preceded it," he adds, "I for
one do not believe. . . . I would as soon have a winking Madonna
. . . as the doubtful experiments . . . which the high priests of modern
science are applauded with one voice for trying to palm off upon their
devotees" (213). His final hope is that "the work of the just men
made perfect through suffering that have gone before" (214) will ease
the lot of mankind.

The *Spectator*[12] reviewed *Ex Voto* at length, calling it a "singular book" with "vivid descriptions" and "strange and fascinating illustrations." "Its startling ideas," the reviewer says, "amounting often to discoveries and new departures in the world of religious art—its criticisms, full of knowledge and originality, if also of a certain mocking spirit which destroys the effect of it for some minds—this book, with all its peculiarities, is certainly a striking contribution to literature of the kind."

Articles on Art

During this period of his life Butler engaged in other controversies and defenses of unpopular or even lost causes. Responding to the rough treatment given him by critics throughout his career up to now, he rushed in to defend neglected or overlooked figures, feeling somehow that he alone was the St. George who must fight off the specialist and professional dragons. He was seeking also by other means to turn his failure as a painter into success as a student of art. Nevertheless, it is hard to understand why he now spent such energy and so much time in research and in attempts to persuade others of the rightness of his insights when he must have known all along that they did not care what he thought. But the layman reading these books and articles now finds many of the arguments so convincing that he wonders why they were almost totally rejected and ignored when they appeared.

In 1886 Butler published in the *Athenaeum* (20 February and 15 May) two articles on "Portraits of Gentile and Giovanni Bellini" (*Collected Essays*, 2, 151–56) in which he attempted to defend the genuineness of a Louvre painting that had recently been ascribed to Cariani. He noted the age of the previously accepted tradition that the picture was by Gentile Bellini, and also expressed his belief that the same two heads appeared in the Bellini picture *St. Mark's Sermon*, in a fresco by Titian, and in Marziale's picture *The Circumcision*. But his researches on this subject failed to impress the experts, and the picture is now called *Portraits d'hommes* and is still ascribed to Cariani.

In November 1888 the *Universal Review* published Butler's article on "The Sanctuary of Montrigone." In this article he is still looking for additional works to be identified as Tabachetti's. The lightly bantering tone in which he discusses such questions as mothers-in-law and medieval methods of eating eggs gives the essay an odd charm. It illustrates Butler's conviction that "it is not until faith begins to be weak that it fears an occasional lighter treatment of semi-sacred subjects" (*Collected Essays,* 2, 159).

Over a long period Butler had been having a controversy with the authorities of the museum at Basel concerning the authenticity of a drawing there by which he was first struck in 1871, and which he had endeavored to copy in 1884, 1885, and 1886. In his study of this drawing he became gradually convinced that it was a Holbein original. The museum authorities had listed it as an 1850 copy. On the evidence Butler provided, they listed it as a 1624 copy, but refused to admit it to be by Holbein. After writing a long letter to the *Academy* (23 October 1886) and after issuing two printed cards of the picture, Butler presented his entire case in an article on "L'Affaire Holbein-Rippel" in the *Universal Review* (November 1889). The article is an excellent example of the painstaking work he could do on such a subject.

In the December 1888 issue of the *Universal Review* appeared "A Medieval Girl School," in which Butler gives a gently humorous account of the chapels at Oropa. Again he decries the seriousness with which the English take their religion. Again he protests the blindness of tradition that shuts people's eyes to things of value because they have not been recognized by others. "[There] is no hedge," he says, "so thick or so thorny as the dulness of culture" (*Collected Essays,* 2, 204). He evinces a very Victorian desire to have a picture tell a story, and he enjoys figuring out what that story is. He also makes a striking statement of the attitude of scientists and churchmen toward truth:

It seems to me that in the matter of accuracy, priests and men of science whether lay or regular on the one hand, and plain people . . . on the other, are trying to play a different game, and fail to understand one another because they do not see that their objects are not the same. The cleric and the man of science (who is only the cleric in his latest development) are trying to develop a throat with two distinct passages—one that shall refuse to pass even the smallest gnat, and the other that shall gracefully gulp even the largest camel; whereas we men of the street desire but one throat, and are content that this shall swallow nothing bigger than a pony. (*Collected Essays,* 2, 210)

And he urges the Church to give up her literal beliefs so that intelligent people may join her.

Science Lectures and Articles

It would be a mistake to assume that Butler's writing about art meant that he had given up his battle to win a place for his theories about evolution or had stopped following the publications in this field. In fact, he was fascinated to see that, without mentioning his work, more and more writers and theorists were moving slowly in his direction.

In 1882 he was twice invited to lecture at the Working Men's College, and he chose memory as his subject. In 1887 he lectured again, this time "On the Genesis of Feeling." In this lecture he views the nervous system as a kind of complex telegraph network evolved by evolutionary processes for the purpose of transmitting feelings which, originating as a sense of shock, had evolved into a complex basis for thought—"feeling being only opinion writ small" (*Collected Essays,* 1, 193). He also argues that, just as words are arbitrary names of things, so also are ideas, since they too "have reference to our own convenience rather than to the thing itself" (204). "Will, effort, and deliberation have been essential factors in the formation of the idea from its earliest inception to its most matured form," he says, thus taking his stand with the evolutionary positivists of the nineteenth century. "I make use and disuse," he adds, "the main factor of mental as much as of physical evolution" (206). At the lecture's conclusion he asks: "What is the secret of learning to feel rightly?" and replies, "To wish to feel more accurately is the first stage. . . . And the second is like unto it: try to do so." So, he concludes, "Never say that you feel a thing unless you feel it distinctly; and if you do not feel it distinctly, say at once that you do not as yet quite know your own mind" (209–10).

In March 1887 Butler lectured on "The Subdivisions of the Organic World into Animal and Vegetable." This lecture, later printed in *Science and Art* (May, June 1887), suggests that the existence of two main branches of living beings can be traced to the opposing philosophies (1) of lying in wait for what comes to one (vegetable) or (2) of going hunting for what one wants (animal). In addition to developing this thesis, the lecture contains many effective remarks upon the principles to be followed in formulating any theory—in not pushing too far beyond common sense; in realizing that in the last analysis everything, except for the frozen thoughts of the inorganic realm, ends in contradiction; and in being aware of the real difficulty of opening up again a discussion that has been so long settled as to be a part of our unconscious minds. The essay reveals Butler's speculative powers at their best.

The April, May, and June 1890 issues of the *Universal Review* contained three articles by Butler on "The Deadlock in Darwinism." He begins by restating the differences between Lamarckianism and Darwinism, demonstrating once more that Charles Darwin had frequently hedged and had often adopted the theory basic to Lamarckianism that variations occur because of the desire for them. He finds examples of similar hedging in Alfred Russell Wallace, the co-discoverer of the "Survival of the Fittest" theory. The most interesting part of the article is the discussion of August Weismann, the German biologist who had just advanced the claim that germ cells are passed on unchanged from generation to generation. In Weismann, as in Darwin and Wallace, Butler finds ambiguity. Weismann writes that "the assumption that changes induced by external conditions in the organism as a whole are communicated to the germ-cells" may "occasionally" prove correct. Butler calls this letting in the thin edge of the wedge, which is all that Lamarckianism needs (*Collected Essays,* 2: 36–37). He says of these writers: "I become like a fly in a windowpane. I see the sunshine and freedom beyond, and buzz up and down their pages, ever hopeful to get through them to the fresh air without, but ever kept back by a mysterious something, which I feel but cannot grasp or see" (39). This "something" is the Darwinian refusal to admit that he ascribes variations to anything but chance and accident.

In the last of the three articles he restates his *Life and Habit* theory, and points out that some of the leading biologists have begun to adopt it but that no one has explored its implications. "Why," he asks, "have so many of our leaders shown such a strong hankering after the theory, if there is nothing in it?" (56).

In March 1890 Butler again lectured at the Working Men's College, this time on "Thought and Language." He attacked Max Müller's contention (*Science of Language,* 1861, and *Three Lectures on the Science of Language,* 1889) that no thought exists without language and that animals are incapable of reason. He gives many examples of the language of gesture and expression and of animal reasoning; then he comments: "After all, a professor, whether of philology, psychology, biology, or any other ology, is hardly the kind of person to whom we should appeal on such an elementary question as that of animal intelligence and language. We might as well ask a botanist to tell us whether grass grows, or a meteorologist to tell us if it has left off raining" (82).[13]

Butler realized that his theory of evolution would tolerate no gap between animals and men in ability to communicate and reason, and the idea was abhorrent as well to his own intuitive sympathy with others—for, as he says, if we will not admit that animals can think, why should we believe that other people beside ourselves can either? In addition, the idea went against his recognition of unconscious processes. Describing two fighting pugilists, he says: "the main part of the fighting will be done without any internal concomitance of articulated phrases. Yet we cannot doubt that their action . . . is guided by intelligence and reason . . . reason or thought, for the most part, flies along over the heads of words, working its own mysterious way in paths that are beyond our ken" (86–87).

Two Humorous Articles

In a lighter vein, he wrote two pieces for the *Universal Review* in 1888 and 1889. In "Quis Desiderio . . . ?" he bewails the disappearance from the reference shelves of the British Museum of Dr. John Frost's *Lives of Eminent Christians,* which for a dozen years he had used as a writing desk. "It is not the custom of modern writers," says Butler, "to refer to the works to which they are most deeply indebted, . . . but it is to this book alone that I have looked for support during many years of literary labour, and it is round this to me invaluable volume that all my own have, page by page, grown up" (*Collected Essays,* 2, 106). Somehow, he gets onto the subject of Wordsworth's Lucy and speculates that "Wordsworth had murdered her, either by cutting her throat or smothering her, in concert, perhaps, with his friends Southey and Coleridge; and, if he had thus found himself released from an engagement which had become irksome to him, or possibly from the threat of an action for breach of promise, then there is not a syllable in the poem with which he crowns his crime that is not alive with meaning" (108). In the second of the two articles, "The Aunt, the Nieces, and the Dog," he reproduces some old letters he found among his grandfather's papers and some that Jones had lent him, and he revels in their triviality and in their illiterate spelling. He concludes with some Erewhonian remarks about the important function of universities in keeping down the amount of originality in society, the obverse side of his more usual appeal to each of us to see the world with his own eyes. "Our public schools and universities," he says, "play the beneficent part in our social scheme that cattle do in forests: they browse the seedlings down and prevent the growth of all but the luckiest and sturdiest. . . . If a young man, in spite of every effort to fit him with blinkers, will insist on getting rid of them, he must do so at his own risk'' (128).

The Life and Letters of Dr. Samuel Butler

In 1888 the Shrewsbury Archaeological Society asked Butler to prepare a memoir of his grandfather, the headmaster of Shrewsbury School and Bishop of Lichfield (1774–1839). His sisters sent Butler the bishop's correspondence, and it so intrigued him that he soon decided to write a full-length study rather than the forty to eighty pages the society had requested. As he read the letters entrusted to him, Butler found in his grandfather a person he could heartily admire: his manliness, calm self-possession, scholarliness, and kindliness appealed to him immensely. He was soon more in sympathy with the straightforwardness of the period—having more in it as it did of the eighteenth than of the nineteenth century—than he was with his contemporary world. He was sorry that he had been as hard on George Pontifex in his novel as he had, for he had created this character in accordance with the impression he had of his grandfather at that time. He wished to revise that part of the novel, although he never did so.[14]

The clarity and directness of the style of writing in those days delighted him immensely—it was like his own; and the vigor of the controversies and the trials and tribulations and successes of Dr. Butler gave him a vision of a life he felt he would have loved. His aim in writing the book soon came to be not to pass judgment or to explain but simply to set as much of the material before the reader as he possibly could. He wished to show not only his grandfather as he had lived, but also the school and the church of his time. He packed his book full of letters and copious extracts from all kinds of documents, and it grew to immense size. He later said that writing this book had taught him more than anything else he had ever done.[15] The men of his grandfather's generation, he felt, were genuine and honest; they understood the value of common sense and sound judgment; and they were not frightened by inroads of speculation. Though open-minded, they possessed a conviction of order and of their own worth that was not shattered by the advent of the imperious scientific spirit. Butler was at home with them. They represented the Towneley spirit, but in a context of sensitivity and scholarliness, service and faith not stultified by false culture and pretense.

During 1889 Butler spent much time gathering material for this biography; he collected additional letters, interviewed dozens of people who remembered his grandfather, and left no stone unturned in his investigations.[16] But his researches took longer than he had anticipated, and five years passed before he finally sent the manuscript to a publisher. He had begun to realize by now that his books might succeed better if he could get them printed at a publisher's risk rather than by underwriting them himself. He engaged a literary agent, and tried his best to find a commercial outlet for the study of his grandfather and for the works on Homer to which we will shortly come. He was unsuccessful, however. *The Life and Letters of Dr. Samuel Butler* was rejected by the Oxford and Cambridge presses, by John Murray, and by others. Finally, Butler cut it by a third and commissioned John Murray to produce it.[17]

The Life and Letters is a leisurely biography, stuffed with characteristic passages revealing the spirit of the late eighteenth and early nineteenth centuries. A storehouse of all sorts of odd information, it makes fascinating reading because of its concreteness. We see all through it that Butler revered and loved his material and his grandfather so much that he did not wish to touch them, but rather longed to see them just as they were. In no other volume does Butler obtrude himself upon his reader so little as in this. And here may be the greatest obtrusion of all, for we cannot escape the reverential atmosphere. The method he uses is the antithesis of Lytton Strachey's. The book is in a sense a storehouse of history rather than an interpretation. For example, Butler presents a vast supply of facts about the English public-school system, but nowhere does he evaluate or criticize. We might conclude, if we knew nothing else from his pen, that he regarded the system as well-nigh perfect. Had his encounters with the brash presumptuousness of the scientific spirit persuaded him that classical education, like the church, was indeed better than recent developments? A spirit of enlightened and kindly conservatism pervades this little-read biography. It does not forecast the renewed satire of *Erewhon Revisited*.

The critics were at last really pleased with something Butler had done. The *Spectator*[18] regretted that he had reduced the work from twelve hundred to eight hundred pages. The *Athenaeum*[19] gave the book a five-column, front-page review. "We have to thank Mr. Butler," it said, "for a really interesting work—one all the better for being free from the conventional tone of the ordinary biographer. . . . The book is compiled with Mr. Butler's well-known skill." The *Academy,*[20] on the other hand, called the work too long and not interpretative enough. Queen Victoria, however, had her thanks conveyed to Butler and he received many letters of congratulation.[21] For once, he had attacked no prejudices, touched no sore spots. The results were gratifying, but not what his deepest genius continued to require of him. He would not long remain so civilized.

Chapter Seven
Renewed Discoveries

Jones relates that a mention of the *Odyssey* in Canon Ainger's book on Lamb suggested to Butler the idea of an oratorio on Ulysses. His studies for this musical work led him in 1891 to reread the *Odyssey* in the original.[1] Of this rereading Butler remarks: "The more I reflected on the words, so luminous and so transparent, the more I felt a darkness behind them that I must pierce before I could see the heart of the writer—and this was what I wanted; for art is only interesting in so far as it reveals an artist" (*The Authoress,* 6). In an attempt to arouse the interest of others in Homer, he gave another address at the Working Men's College in 1892 on "The Humour of Homer" and had it published in the *Eagle* for March of that year. It is an example of the spirit of paganism and laughter bringing a subject to life, but is designed to shock and annoy traditional classical scholars.

The Authoress of the Odyssey

With characteristic thoroughness, Butler set to work to translate the *Odyssey,* searching as he did so for anything that would answer his vague questionings. "It was not till I got to Circe," he tells us, "that it flashed upon me that I was reading the work not of an old man but of a young woman" (8). This intuitive insight having seized him, he gathered all the internal evidence he could to back it up. In addition, he added insult to injury by emulating Heinrich Schliemann. "He made a list of the various natural features of Scheria, as detailed in the poem, and set about looking in the map for some spot that should satisfy all the requirements."[2] This spot he concluded to be Trapani and Mount Eryx in Sicily, and he promptly announced his discovery in two letters to the *Athenaeum.*[3]

Not since his work on *Life and Habit* had anything excited him so much. For the last ten years of his life he threw himself heart and soul into a defense of these two "discoveries," and he exhausted himself with travel and work in the process. His detached and humorous observation of life almost deserted him at times. He was so far from being a Laodicean or a sideline-sitter that he had to remind himself constantly of the value of the *surtout point de zèle* doctrine to keep control of his enthusiasms. He claimed, of course, that his proposals were tentative and that he awaited refutation by the experts. But by this time he should have known that the experts would greet him with silent contempt as an interloper whose ideas were beneath their consideration. Once again, he was trying to arouse them by presenting a mass of evidence carefully worked up after their own fashion and then by proving that they would not give it a fair day in court.

Not that he did not win some converts. Jones tells us in his introduction to the Shrewsbury Edition of *The Authoress* that Lord Grimthorpe, Justice Wills, and George Bernard Shaw were convinced (xxvii); and more recently Robert Graves says, "While working on an explanatory dictionary of Greek myths, I found Butler's arguments for a western Sicilian setting and for a female authorship irrefutable."[4] But this is small success for a project of which Butler himself said, "Nothing has ever interested me (except, of course, Handel) so much as this *Odyssey* business has done; it is far the finest piece of good fortune that ever happened to me, and I find it all the sweeter for the strong displeasure it has aroused in academic circles."[5] The man was incorrigible. He was going to prove that the complacent experts of his "cultured" society were not what they pretended to be, even if it killed him to do so.

His excitement is pathetically revealed in a passage in Jones's biography. "He found scarcely any one in England who took any intelligent interest in the subject. . . . He used, therefore, to talk about the *Odyssey* to me, coming to my rooms evening after evening, inventing the objections which his opponents ought to have raised, considering them, adopting them tentatively, and finally embracing them with such ardour that he crushed them to pieces." When Jones tried to interest him in other subjects, Butler would listen politely, with his mind far away with Nausicaä, and then return to the discussion of the *Odyssey*. "This incessant dwelling upon one subject at last began to produce its effect. . . . [On his way home] he . . . felt giddy and was obliged to hold on to the railings to keep himself from falling."[6]

The main argument of *The Authoress of the Odyssey* is sustained by such a wealth of detailed reference to the *Odyssey* and the *Iliad* that it becomes more and more compelling. Butler was sincere in his contention that he wanted nothing so much as an answer to the reasoning that led him to his convictions. "What can it matter to me where the Odyssey was written, or whether it was written by a man or a woman? From the bottom of my heart I can say truly that I do not care about the way in which these points are decided, but I do care, and very greatly, about knowing which way they are decided by sensible people who have considered what I have urged in this book" (281). The trouble was that the sort of points he urged, as in his books on evolution where he dwelt on unconscious memory and the purpose of change, were not the sort with which specialists engaged themselves, then or now. Ennis Rees opens the introduction to his translation of the *Iliad* by blandly remarking that the *Iliad* and the *Odyssey* are "largely the work of one great poet, or perhaps two . . ."[7] as though it did not really matter which. T. E. Shaw on the other hand, like Butler, tries "to deduce the author from his self-betrayal in the work," but comes up with completely opposite conclusions to Butler's: he finds "a bookworm, no longer young, living from home, a mainlander, city-bred and domestic" with "infuriating male condescension towards inglorious woman."[8]

In *The Authoress,* as in *Unconscious Memory,* Butler gives much attention to the steps in his own thinking that led to his unorthodox conclusions. It is certainly true that for him the "truth" is always such a human thing that it can only be fully realized in terms of the personal, individual insights leading up to it. Butler is not being egotistical but faithful to his own convictions in giving the biography of his speculations. Nevertheless, one can speculate that he was unaware of the "real" reasons for what he was doing, as most of us generally are, and that in ascribing the *Odyssey* to a woman it is possible that he was unconsciously doing penance for his suppression of the desire to have a wife. Yet supposing he had known this, his work might have been only the richer for the knowledge. As he follows the *Odyssey* step by step, discussing detail after detail, we are forced to ask ourselves whether we know the poem nearly as well as he does (he had memorized large parts of it), and also to ask what counterproposals we might supply to each argument he advances. There is much reading into the poem of Butler's own attitudes toward life: toward men and women, and what they are likely to do and not do, as there is in T. E. Shaw's remarks; toward what is humorous and toward the possible ways in which an artist can create his art. We are not so inclined today as the Victorians were to believe that "art is only interesting in so far as it reveals the artist,"[9] or to worry about the exact geographical details of an ancient poem or about the sex of its author. We believe that we do enough if we study a work of art for its internal consistency and beauty. Dickens discovered from internal evidence that George Eliot was a woman, but then he could verify the truth of his discovery by asking her publisher. Perhaps in the future scholarship will once again become interested in the sort of issues Butler found so fascinating.

Alison Booth says that although Butler's Homeric studies are passed over by most students of Butler and of Victorian thought and are "an aberration in classical scholarship," as criticism *The Authoress* is still "of vital interest."[10] "When Samuel Butler sets out in quest of the source of the *Odyssey* he is once again [as in *Erewhon*] turning his back on his contemporaries, yet as always he carries the spirit of his age with him to a strange frontier."[11] In Butler, this writer believes, as in Walter Pater, "a creative spirit transcends the culture that it helps to reshape . . . if this spirit is gemlike in Pater, in Butler it is bricks and mortar."[12] But unfortunately Butler's emphasis on the "problems" the *Odyssey* poses makes us read the poem as "a scientific investigation," as his translation turns it into a Victorian novel. He "dissects the *Odyssey*, displays its matter in detail, and reassembles it as [his own] immortal discovery."[13] Although Butler assumes that he "knows human nature better and ancient Sicily almost as well as the authoress" and has indeed "in effect written the *Odyssey* himself,"[14] he has nevertheless "extended the scope of creative criticism" by his endeavors.[15] Alison Booth's shrewd and insightful analysis thus suggests that *The Authoress of the Odyssey* is a more powerful work than almost anyone except Butler himself has ever thought it was.

The *Saturday Review*[16] made a comment on *The Authoress* that Butler must have appreciated: "We do not disdain Mr. Butler's book. It is written with great vivacity, and if it takes a number of readers to the pure and beautiful text of the 'Odyssey' and induces them to treat it, not as a dusty school-book, but as a living and sensitive portion of literature, its action will not have been in vain." And *Notes and Queries*[17] gave the book a really favorable review, calling Butler "far too fine and accurate a scholar to be calmly pooh-poohed." It added, "There are . . . some editors of Greek texts to whom we may justly look for a response, seeing that the points raised can no longer be ignored." The response was not forthcoming. But it is good that at least one reviewer saw the issue about which Butler felt so strongly.

Translating Homer

His renewed study of the *Iliad* and the *Odyssey* drew Butler's attention to the fact that there was no English translation of the two poems into simple, straightforward, contemporary language. "He who would write a translation like those of the Elizabethans," he said, "must above all else avoid Elizabethanisms."[18] His conviction was that "a translation should depart hardly at all from the modes of speech current in the translator's own times" (*The Iliad,* xiii). He wanted to make a translation "with the same benevolent leaning (say) towards Tottenham Court Road that Messrs. Butcher and Lang have shown towards Wardour Street."[19] In his *Note-Books* Butler says: "If you wish to preserve the spirit of a dead author, you must not skin him, stuff him, and set him up in a case. . . . The difference between the Andrew Lang manner of translating the Odyssey and mine is that between making a mummy and a baby. He tries to preserve a corpse . . . whereas I try to originate a new life and one that is instinct (as far as I can effect this) with the spirit though not the form of the original" (197).

Choosing at random a passage from Butcher and Lang's *Odyssey* translation and from Butler's we can see what he was attempting: (Book 2, line 208ff.): "Then wise Telemachus answered him, saying: 'Eurymachus, and ye others, that are lordly wooers, I entreat you no more concerning this nor speak thereof, for the gods have knowledge of it now and all the Acheans,' " which in Butler appears much more simply and clearly as: "Then Telemachus said, 'Eurymachus, and you other suitors, I shall say no more, and entreat you no further, for the gods and the people of Ithaca now know my story.' " For further comparison, a verse translation done by Albert Cook in the 1960s goes as follows: "Then sound-minded Telemachus addressed him in answer, / 'Eurymachos, and all the rest of you noble suitors, / I will not implore you about this or speak out any more. / Already the gods know this, and all the Achaians.' " If Butler's translations suffer for the modern reader from being touched by Victorian colloquialism, perhaps it is only the beginning of "the mosses and lichens which Time will grow" (*The Iliad of Homer,* xiii). The Butler translations are still very readable and have been widely circulated.[20]

The *Academy,*[21] furious about the new translation, called it "woefully superfluous" and claimed that by discarding archaic expressions Butler had ruined the whole tone of the poem. But the *Athenaeum*[22] cast its vote for "the increased naturalness and simplicity of Butler" and was grateful for the "vivid and direct prose" reminiscent of Hobbes. *Notes and Queries*[23] said: "No student of Homer more zealous, accomplished and devoted than he can our country boast. . . . We know no English work which will give the average English reader a better insight into Homer." But only 157 copies of the *Iliad* translation were sold in the first year after its publication.[24]

Shakespeare's Sonnets Reconsidered

In 1895, Henry Festing Jones tells us,[25] Butler began a close study of Shakespeare's *Sonnets,* for he believed that internal evidence might unlock their secret, just as he was confident it had unlocked for him that of the *Odyssey.* Disagreeing with Jones's dating, Hans-Peter Breuer concludes that Butler's real interest came not in 1895 but in 1897, close on the heels of Charles Paine Pauli's death, at which time Butler first learned of the affluence of this puzzling man.[26] Pauli, for whom Butler had had a great affection and who had encouraged Butler's literary work, had always let Butler think that without his help of £200 yearly and frequent meals he would be destitute. Ross Stuart speculates that Pauli may have meant so much to Butler by the skill of his literary advice and the encouragement of his wordly competence that he was well worth an annual retainer fee and in fact accepted his stipend as he would have accepted any professional payment. After their return to London, however, Stuart speculates, Butler "no longer marvelled at Pauli; he vied with him for dominance" and when Butler finally withdrew his affection, Pauli collapsed, more sinned against than sinning. Although Butler was "a pioneer in the study of the unconscious," he never fathomed either Pauli's motives or his own.[27] This analysis suggests, if true, that although there may be some connection between Pauli and Butler's interpretation of the *Sonnets,* it is not as simple as either Breuer or Muggeridge thought. Breuer believes that Butler, quite unaware that he was doing so, read into Shakespeare's sonnet sequence a version of his own bitter disappointment at Pauli's growing coldness toward him, and Malcolm Muggeridge believes that Butler's reading of the *Sonnets* reflects his own homosexual experience.[28]

Shakespeare's Sonnets Reconsidered and in Part Rearranged was published in 1899. There had been much speculation about the identity of Mr. W. H.; about the dating of the poems; and about individual passages, which Butler summarizes and discusses. But no one had ever had the audacity to go through the sonnets detail by detail and to pretend that he could fit them together into a coherent whole. The Victorians were embarrassed by the sonnets and apologetic, as is well exemplified in Edward Dowden's gingerly discussion.[29] They preferred to steer clear of the sort of conclusion that Butler drew, in comparing the sonnets with the *Iliad:* "Whereas the love of Achilles for Patroclus depicted by the Greek poet is purely English, absolutely without taint or alloy of any kind, the love of the English poet for Mr. W. H. was, though only for a short time, more Greek than English" (145).

Part of Butler's argument, though, turns on a puzzlingly literal interpretation of Sonnet 33. He deduces from the preceding sonnets that Mr. W. H. "in concert with others" laid a trap for the poet, and that he was "made to 'travel forth without' that 'cloak' which, if he had not been lured, we may be sure that he would not have discarded. Hardly had he laid the cloak aside before he was surprised according to a preconcerted scheme, and very probably roughly handled, for we find him lame soon afterwards . . . and apparently not fully recovered a twelvemonth later" (82–83). Butler is certain that the sonnets must be very early works because they thus record the indiscretions of youth, which could not be forgiven an older man. He argues that Sonnet 107 refers to the defeat of the Spanish Armada, and from this he deduces that the poems belong to the years 1585–88. Leslie Hotson, Robert Bridges, and Ivor Winters agree that the poems are early work.[30]

How, we wonder, could Butler feel so confident of the unlikely story he *makes* these poems tell? This book, like his other literary detective work, shows evidence of much careful labor, and it explores with skill the defective arguments of many previous scholars. But, having memorized the whole sonnet sequence, having meditated on it for months, and having examined in the British Museum what others had written about the *Sonnets,* Butler draws from them a story built on a chain of such tenuous inferences and doubtful interpretations that the reader gasps with amazement.[31]

If we do not feel Butler's driving compulsion to get at a story behind the *Sonnets,* or even believe that there may never have been a story at all, Butler has this to say to us: "It may be asked, Why have a story, when the one which Q alone permits is throughout painful and in parts repulsive? Many, indeed, say 'Read the Sonnets if you like, but do not go below their surface; let their music and beauty of expression be enough.' I do not write for these good people, nor are they likely

to read me; I therefore pass them by at as wide a distance as I can"
(100).

Perhaps he has a point, but we cannot accept the over-literal interpretation he provides. Nevertheless his book has done us a service: it
has made us think about the *Sonnets* more carefully than we ever had
before. We would agree with the Poet Laureate Robert Bridges, to
whom Butler sent a copy of his book (he was the brother of Butler's
sister's husband), who wrote Butler that "The absence of rise and fall
of feeling with the poem, gives to your book (at first reading) an
uncongenial dryness almost like a want of poetic sympathy. . . . I
willingly recognize that no one has brought the matter into so clear a
light as you have done—you are always perspicuous—and nothing but
good can come of such conscientious work as yours."[32] We would also
agree with the *Academy*[33] that it is a work that "no serious student
can afford to neglect," and with *Notes and Queries*[34] that "all that Mr.
Butler says is scholarly, ingenious and worthy of attention." But still
we wonder why he pushed so fast and went so far. Was he desperate
for one great discovery before he died that would be his acknowledged
child—the world having cruelly cast aside all he had so far laid on
the altar of immortality?

Chapter Eight
Alpha and Omega

On 14 May 1902 Butler wrote from Naples, Italy, to friends that he was gravely ill and was going back to London at once. "You will not forget the pretty roundness of my literary career!" he wrote. "Alpha *Erewhon*, omega *Erewhon Revisited*."[1] Later, back in London, he said to Jones: "First I write *Erewhon*—that is my opening subject, then after modulating freely through all my other books and the music and so on, I return gracefully to my original key and publish *Erewhon Revisited*."[2] In this alphabetical and musical summary of his career he does not mention his revision of the 1872 *Erewhon* or the elaborate notebooks he had been keeping beginning in 1874.

Erewhon Revisited

Since 1872 the ideas of *Erewhon* and plans for *Erewhon Revisited* had never been far from Butler's mind. His notes show a gradual accumulation of suggestions to be added to the *Erewhon* material. In 1896 he told Fisher Unwin that he had often thought of writing a sequel to his early book, and in 1900 he began work on it.[3] When, in the spring of 1901, Longmans declined to publish the newly completed volume because it would give offense "to his connection among the High Anglican party,"[4] Butler wrote to George Bernard Shaw, who had praised the *Odyssey* theory when Butler addressed the Fabian Society ("not, heaven forbid, that I belong to or have any sympathy with the Fabian Society"[5]). He asked Shaw what publisher he would recommend, and Shaw promptly persuaded Grant Richards to undertake the book and also to publish a revised edition of *Erewhon*. Thus Richards became the first publisher to assume a financial risk for a book by Butler.[6]

In spite of the author's disavowal in his preface of any such intent (xxiv), *Erewhon Revisited* is the most biting and direct attack on religion of all of Butler's works. Meditating on what the Erewhonians might make of the escape of the hero of *Erewhon* in a balloon, Butler conceived the idea of presenting the growth of a new religion in a way that would satirize the origins of Christianity itself and the origins as well of all religions based on miracles. He has his hero, now named Higgs, return thirty years later to the country he had discovered to find that it is in the grip of a religious cult developed by skillful manipulators who do not themselves believe what they say, but are perfectly willing to lie to the people to get control over them. This religion is based on "the apparently miraculous ascent of a remarkable stranger into the heavens with an earthly bride" (xxiii) and has developed all the traditional trappings: a "bible" containing the recorded sayings of Higgs while in Erewhon and much that he never said; miracles such as the arrival of four flying horses to take the balloon aloft back to Higgs's home in the sun; the dogma that Higgs is the son of the sun-god (hence the religion is called "Sunchildism"); and miraculous articles such as some coprolites said to be the droppings of the flying horses. There are even schisms in the debate whether the Sunchild wore his clothes buttoned up in front or behind.

Butler satirizes the High Churchmen, Broad Churchmen, and Evangelicals of his day as well as the various types of intellectuals who move in university circles. There is the lukewarm Dr. Downie, who really damages the new religion by his lip service to it. There is the hard-boiled realist Hanky, Professor of Worldly Wisdom at Bridgeford, the city of the people who are above suspicion, who gets Higgs's gold from him by assuring him that it is not gold (the *Life and Habit* theory?), even though Higgs soon after steals it back again, and who burns the clothes Higgs left in Erewhon when they were entrusted to him for study like the experts who destroy the evidence in an argument. And there is the scholarly but namby-pamby Panky, who insists on an amendment of one of the Sunchild's most famous sayings, making it into "Forgive us our trespasses, but do not forgive those who trespass against us" (41) as alone making sense.

Although the satire lacks subtlety, it is still effective. But Butler plants upon it the insights of his later years, his growing willingness to accept things as they are as preferable to the biologically dangerous upheavals of a real revolution, thus implying that this new religious cult he has been satirizing may be all for the best. He is convinced that if the religion is suddenly exposed for the fraud that it is and is swept aside, something far worse would take its place. Higgs says:

"Better a corrupt church than none at all. . . . Those who in my country would step into the church's shoes are as corrupt as the church, and more exacting. They are also more dangerous, for the masses distrust the church, and are on their guard against aggression, whereas they do not suspect the doctrinaires and faddists, who, if they could, would interfere in every concern of our lives. . . . What I have said is nine-tenths of it rotten and wrong, but it is the most practicable rotten and wrong that I can suggest, seeing into what a rotten and wrong state of things you have drifted." (221)

Knowing of Butler's growing conviction that life is a series of compromises and knowing too that he feared that scientists, by their ability to use double-talk and to mislead the public, could finally persuade them that existence is nothing but the operation of blind cause and effect, we understand Higgs's warning; but *Erewhon Revisited* does not spell this out. Its telling satire is, after all, of the church, not of those "who would step into the church's shoes." Higgs himself feels the conflict within him between his idealism and his knowledge that he must accept what is "rotten and wrong." Reason tells him that he should hew to the truth, but instinct advocates compromise. "This was the strongest internal conflict that I ever remember to have felt, and it was at the end of it that I perceived the first, but as yet faint symptoms of that sickness from which I shall not recover" (66).

Butler here in a way denies the thrust of his whole life, of the energy and drive that had forced him to probe for truth in *Erewhon, The Fair Haven,* and *Life and Habit,* even though he had always been aware of ambivalence. Higgs is relieved by his unheroic decision. "The giddiness which had for some seconds compelled him to lay hold of the first thing he could catch at in order to avoid falling, passed away." (66–67). But on returning to England he is a changed man; he falls sick and dies. So it is evident that he cannot accept the compromise that the aging Butler seems to recommend. Thus *Erewhon Revisited* becomes an embodiment of Butler's development and indeed is, as he expressed it with a touch of sadness, the Omega of his career, as *Erewhon* itself was the Alpha.

The author invents an exciting plot, giving the book something of the feeling of a Tom Swift adventure yarn,[7] and by this plot to some extent draws attention away from the satirical implications of the text. Higgs's life is endangered by the schemings of Hanky who actually arranges to have Higgs burned at the stake at the close of the dedication ceremony of a cathedral built to honor the Sunchild (Higgs himself). Yram and George, Higgs's son by Yarm, the jailkeeper's daughter, meanwhile scheme desperately to avoid this eventuality and, by arresting Higgs for poaching before Hankey's church officials seize him, save his life in the nick of time. All of this is cleverly worked out, the threat of being drowned in the Blue Pool always hanging over Higgs's head.

There are other facets to this interesting book. In the ranger George, Higgs finds someone he can totally love. This young man has the physical beauty and the unconscious competence in all he does that Butler longed for, and represents the perfect son he might himself have had. There is undisguised emotion in Butler's account of the relations between Higgs and his son George. George declares to his father, whom he does not yet recognize, that, if the Sunchild would return and publicly announce that he was not divine, he would forgive him and accept him as his father. Would Butler have loved his own father if he had had the courage to tell the truth about what he really believed? The events of the story are arranged to give Higgs a chance to make this admission, and he thus wins for himself the devotion of a son. In this episode Butler's longing for an honest father is as clearly implied as his longing for a son appears to be.

In this dual relationship lies the deepest theme of the story. It has the quality of some of Butler's poetry—warm, strong, and full of feeling—for example, his "In Memoriam" to Hans Faesch, "Out, out, out into the night," (*Note-Books,* 422ff.). There is strong emotion in all of Butler's work, though his clever wit, self-mockery, and bravado hide it from the casual reader. In this idea of a returning divinity who would renounce the false trappings with which an organized church has clothed him is adumbrated the "Grand Inquisitor" theme Dostoyevski developed in *The Brothers Karamazov.*[8] If "Higgs himself were to return," says Higgs to his son, "he would be killed but not believed" (53). "If he [Christ] were to apply for a divorce [from the Church] on the grounds of cruelty, adultery, and desertion," says Butler in his *Note-Books,* "he would probably get one."[9]

Butler expresses his admiration not only for the honest George. He also loves and respects George's resourceful and clever mother Yram, who is the woman Butler might have married had he found her in Victorian England. With tact and intuition she sees through fraud and insincerity, and gets right to the heart of each problem that faces her. She holds the complete love and affection of her husband the mayor, even though he knows that George is not his son. Naturally, she terrifies the two frauds, Hanky and Panky, as Butler would have liked to terrify the Darwins, Jowetts, Sidney Lees, and Garnetts of his day but never succeeded in doing. She is a more successful Butler, suggesting that his own particular genius had much of the feminine in it.

Another interesting view of *Erewhon Revisited* is suggested by Avron Fleishman:[10] perhaps the "rotten and wrong" compromise that Higgs urges to keep the spirit of Sunchildism alive hides Butler's deeper belief that there is really something in the worship of the sun. Referring to the use of the sun in *The Way of All Flesh*, Fleishman writes: "The hidden suggestion of the text is that Butler is in on the secret because he is a child of the sun himself."[11] and now in revising the early version of himself as the hero of *Erewhon* Butler openly calls him "the Sunchild." This imaginative suggestion further undermines the quality of *Erewhon Revisited* as a satire. Still, the suggestion indicates that the book may have in its longing for a natural religion a unity and consequence not often seen in it, a unity Butler himself claims for it in his preface to the revised edition of *Erewhon* (xviii). Butler's affection for his theory of unconscious memory which he never gave up did indeed tie him and everyone else to the primordial speck of life, making us all children of the sun. Nevertheless, it is impossible to disengage the idea of "Sunchildism" from the scorn with which Higgs, Yarm, and George view it. The satirical portraits of Hanky and Panky (in Erewhonian language Hokus and Pokus reversed, both later elevated to sainthood) are too strong and memorable for us to believe that Butler really wished to advocate the toleration of any religion based on exploitation, conscious fraud, and even crime, any more than he would want us to tolerate a science so based.

Erewhon Revisited is certainly not the variegated performance that *Erewhon* had been. But it has its own inversions of the world we know, just as *Erewhon* had had, such as "Mrs. Tantrums, Nagger, certified by the College of Spiritual Athletics. Terms for ordinary nagging, two shillings and sixpence per hour. Hysterics extra" (62), and the Deformatories where children are taught to lie to prepare them to lead useful lives.

Revision of *Erewhon*

In the revision of *Erewhon* that Butler made at this time to secure a renewed copyright many brilliant touches occur which make it the complex book it is. He added the notion that Erewhonians are subjected to punishment for misfortune, especially in money matters (chapter 10); the examples of Europeans who equate crime with disgrace; the subterfuges by which the Erewhonians pretend to have committed a crime to cover up an illness; and the account of the rigorous training straighteners must undergo. To chapter 11, "Some Erewhonian Trials," he added the trial of a man who was unlucky enough to have lost his wife—"Luck," says the judge, "is the only fit object of human veneration"; and in the next chapter he placed several long discussions of luck. Practically all of chapter 13 on the Erewhonian view of death is new. In the chapter on the Musical Banks (15) a long passage on the relation between religion and the "unconscious instinctive wisdom of millions of past generations" is new, as is the passage on divinity at the end of chapter 16. Most of chapter 22, "The Colleges of Unreason," is also new, including the professor who says "It is not our business to help students to think for themselves," and the discussion of examinations. To "The Book of the Machines" Butler added the discussion of horsepower and of the origin of our admiration for wealth. Chapters 26 and 27 on the rights of animals are entirely new, with their fascinating story, full of multiple meanings, of the student who surreptitiously ate meat, found himself healthier and happier, but was so conscience-stricken that he hanged himself. These changes are considerable enough to place within this early work echoes of Butler's thinking throughout his entire life; but, as we noted earlier, it is well to remember that the echoes were not there in 1872.

Hans-Peter Breuer and Daniel F. Howard in their edition of the 1872 text of *Erewhon*[12] argue that Butler considerably damaged the effectiveness of his satire by the changes he made. They believe that his "self-righteousness" toward the end of his life, "fostered by the frustrations of not having his views taken seriously," was not of a piece with the "detached intellectual playfulness" of the original *Erewhon;* he thus in revision "overlaid *Erewhon* with a quite different sensibility."[13] For example, they write: "by 1901, he no longer felt ambiguous about the social usefulness of the church"[14] and added to his account of the Musical Banks categorical statements such as "the Erewhonian Musical Banks, and perhaps the religious systems of all countries, are now more or less of an attempt to uphold the unfathomable and unconscious instinctive wisdom of millions of past generations, against the comparatively shallow, consciously reasoning, and ephemeral conclusions drawn from that of the last thirty or forty" (119). Also the narrator is no longer "the priggish young man who adds his own ruminations to the Erewhonian paradox," but a "straight man recording what he knows."[15] Butler, these writers point out, always seemed angry about *Erewhon,* and resented that throughout his life it remained his one successful book; indeed, in his preface to the revised edition he calls his revising an "irksome task" (xvii) and says that he is "ashamed of" much of the work (xviii).

These are interesting observations and the scholarly edition of *Erewhon* that backs them up is excellent.[16] But since the narrator of *Erewhon* was never a very consistent figure anyway, the dogmatic touches the older Butler added to his ruminations do not really much change him. After all, Butler did deliberately choose to keep the priggish touches he had originally put in. And many of the additions he made in 1901 enrich rather than damage the fabric of the satire. It is more generous and truer to his lifelong attempt to get at the facts to view the older Butler not as "self-righteous" and grumpily capable of damaging a youthful masterpiece, but rather as a man who has achieved considerable wisdom and is now enriching an earlier work. He does not really "considerably deflate"[17] his satire of the Musical Banks by changing "the possibility that the church is useful" to a categorical suggestion that it is useful; or, for another example, he does not "deny the ambiguity that he had woven into the fabric of his 1872 work" by adding additional examples of the moral treatment of misfortunes. It is not true that in his revisions Butler was " 'prosing' on and on with theories that had long since lost their impact."[18] Readers used to be surprised indeed, but not annoyed, by the fact that *Erewhon* contained so many insights arrived at late in Butler's life, not realizing that they were reading an enriched version. But this distressed no one. The book as it is commonly read in the 1901 version, because that is the only one widely available, is not an oppressively opinionated document.

The Note-Books

Butler had long been in the habit of carrying a small notebook in which to jot down interesting ideas as they came to him. Then, when he was in Canada in 1874, he began systematically weeding out, shortening, rewriting his collection, putting a heading onto each note, and making an index. In 1891 he tackled his notes afresh, and from then on made a practice of spending an hour every morning reediting the notes and keeping the index up to date.[19] In a sense, whether he was aware of it or not, he was belying his own doctrine that simple and direct expression is what comes most easily to us (*Note-Books,* 184–85). The highly conscious labor he put into writing, revising, rearranging his notes proves that simplicity is often hard to achieve. He soon discovered that he hardly ever used these notes, though he thought of them as providing material for future books; but he realized that writing them helped to clear his mind and to fix his ideas in his memory. By the time of his death he had compiled six complete volumes of about 225 large pages each, and he had enough material to fill two more.[20]

Should the notes have been published? In his preface to his second manuscript volume Butler wrote: "It seems to me that [an author] is the worst person . . . to make selections from his own notes, or indeed even, in my case, to write them. I cannot help it. They grew as, with little disturbance, they now stand; they are not meant for publication; the bad ones serve as bread for the jam of the good ones." Yet he adds, "That [the notebooks] will be looked over by not a few I doubt not," and this suggests his awareness that he was writing for more than just himself.

Jones tells us that it was the interest of Desmond MacCarthy that galvanized him into doing something about Butler's notebooks. MacCarthy had browsed in the pressed copy of the notebooks kept in Jones's quarters in case fire should destroy the originals, and when he became editor of the *New Quarterly Magazine* in 1907 he asked Jones to prepare extracts for publication, with the permission of Streatfeild, Butler's literary executor.[21] The published extracts were arranged under specific topics, some of the same ones used later in the book edition, and Jones edited, condensed notes into one, and generally tidied them up for publication. It is evident from the selections made that Jones and MacCarthy had a special interest in the more iconoclastic notes; they both wished to confirm Butler's reputation as a rebellious and unorthodox thinker. In 1912 Jones much enlarged the extracts under twenty-four headings.

The book was enthusiastically received.[22] *The Note-Books of Samuel Butler* was recognized as an important addition to English literature. As much as any book that Butler wrote they bring before us the lucidity of his mind, his uncanny power of expression, and his kindly, quizzical, original way of viewing life, himself, and all his theories. They are a real testimony to the orderliness and constancy of his mind and to his abiding devotion to his work.

Under the opening topic "Lord, What Is Man?" Jones enters some of Butler's comments on mankind, among them the following: "A man is a passing mood coming and going in the mind of his country; he is the twitching of a nerve, a smile, a frown, a thought of shame or honour, as it may happen" (*Note-Books,* Shrewsbury Edition, 1).[23] "A sense of humour keen enough to show a man his own absurdities, as well as those of other people, will keep him from the commission of all sins, or nearly all, save those that are worth committing" (3). "The world may not be particularly wise—still, we know of nothing wiser" (4). "We had better live in others as much as we can if only because we thus live more in the race, which God really does seem to care about a good deal, and less in the individual, to whom, so far as I can see, he is indifferent" (7). "Is life worth living? This is a question for an embryo, not for a man" (9).

The next heading Jones selects is "Elementary Morality." This section begins with the note: "The foundations of morality. These are like other foundations; if you dig too much about them the superstructure will come tumbling down" (17). A long note on the necessity of serving both God and Mammon is included, put together by Jones from a whole series of Butler's entries in various volumes (17–18). There are many examples in this section of Butlerian needling, as for example: "It is the function of vice to keep virtue within reasonable bounds" (21). "Morality turns on whether the pleasure precedes or follows the pain. Thus, it is immoral to get drunk because the headache comes after the drinking, but if the headache came first, and the drunkenness afterwards, it would be moral to get drunk" (22). "To love God is to have good health, good looks, good sense, experience, a kindly nature, and a fair balance of cash in hand" (26). "Heaven is the work of the best and kindest men and women. Hell is the work of prigs, pedants, and professional truth-tellers. The world is an attempt to make the best of both" (28).

The next sections in Jones's volume bring together notes and other materials Butler collected in connection with his books: material for *Erewhon* and for a projected continuation of *Life and Habit,* and material under headings like "Memory and Design," "Vibrations," and "Mind and Matter." A section on "Music, Pictures, and Books" brings together many of his most telling ideas about expression and art. "Thought pure and simple," he writes, "is as near to God as we can get. . . . All the most essential and thinking part of thought is done without words or consciousness. It is not till doubt and consciousness enter that words become possible" (89). "In art," he says, "never try to find out anything, or try to learn anything until the not knowing it has come to be a nuisance to you for some time" (101). "Do not hunt for subjects, let them choose you, not you them" (102). "My books. I never make them; they grow; they come to me and insist on being written, and on being such and such" (102). "If a person is in doubt about this or that in his writing, it will often guide him if he asks himself how it will tell a hundred years hence" (106).

A section on "Handel and Music" follows. Here Butler makes explicit many of his reasons for loving Handel and for disliking Beethoven and Mozart. "A Painter's Views on Painting" develops his ideas on the art that he had tried so hard to make his profession. He explores the value of the apprentice system and the dangers of academicism. "Art," he says, "is at best a dress, important, yet still nothing in comparison with the wearer, and, as a general rule, the less it attracts attention the better" (135). "He is a great artist who can be depended upon not to bark at nothing" (135).

The notes collected under the heading *"Homo Unius Libri"* provide many insights into Butler's attitude toward his own career and reveal the abiding good humor and objectivity that persisted in him in spite of his apparent failures. "He who would propagate an opinion," he says, no doubt thinking of himself, "must begin by making sure of his ground and holding it firmly. There is as little use in trying to breed from weak opinion as from other weak stock, animal or vegetable" (163).

Other headings Jones uses are "Cash and Credit," "Unprofessional Sermons," "Higgledy-Piggledy," and "Written Sketches." In the sketches we see Butler's novelist eye at work, gleaning all sorts of odd scraps of conversation and incident from his daily life that reveal the peculiarities of human nature. "How holy people look when they are sea-sick!" he writes. "There was a patient Parsee near me [on a channel passage] who seemed purified once and for ever from all taint of the flesh. Buddha was a low, worldly-minded, music-hall comic singer in comparison" (257).

The section Jones puts together on "Truth and Convenience" is a compendium of Butler's pragmatic thinking. "There is no such source of error," he writes, "as the pursuit of absolute truth" (302). "There is no permanent absolute unchangeable truth; what we should pursue is the most convenient arrangement of our ideas" (302). "Truth . . . should be played pretty low down—to the pit and gallery rather than the stalls. Pit-truth is more true to the stalls than stall-truth to the pit" (303). "An essential contradiction in terms meets us at the end of every enquiry" (303). In another section on "First Principles" Butler tells us that "We are not won by arguments that we can analyze, but by tone and temper, by the manner which is the man himself" (335).

"It is said," he also comments, that "we can build no superstructure without a foundation of unshakable principles. There are no such principles" (336).

A section on "Rebelliousness" contains some of Butler's notes on God and religion. He says: "If I were to start as a god or a prophet, I think I should take the line: 'Thou shalt not believe in me. Thou shalt not have me for a god. Thou shalt worship any damned thing thou likest except me'" (340). "As an instrument of warfare against vice," he writes, "or as a tool for making virtue, Christianity is a mere flint implement. Christianity is a woman's religion, invented by women and womanish men for themselves" (341). Sections on "Reconciliation," "Death," and "The Life of the World to Come" follow. Finally, Jones concludes his edition of the notebooks with Butler's poetry. In the Shrewsbury Edition he added two sonnets and the words to the cantatas "Narcissus" and "Ulysses."

The notes cannot be adequately abstracted, summarized, or characterized. They must be read by anyone who cares to cross his intellect with something different, with thoughts his "mother did not teach [him] at all, nor [his] father . . . but altogether otherwise."[24] Much thought is embedded in the whimsical, probing fragments of Butler's mind. They are counsels of maturity, courage, and independence. A few characteristic samples from volume 1 of the manuscript notebooks, recently published in their entirety, are the following: "American Dishonesty—Refer it to their Puritan ancestry" (80). "Ultimate Triumph of Good—When we say that we believe in this, we mean that we are cocksure of our own opinions" (88). "God as now generally conceived of is only the last witch" (90). "Truth on any subject is the opinion which either has, or may come to have the whip hand" (94). "There is no such metaphysics as physics in the hands of a scientist who goes too far for his facts" (187). "Reason—if you follow it far enough always leads to conclusions that are contrary to reason" (200).

Such devotion to passing scraps of thought as these notebooks contain, whims of a moment, trivialities even, may seem narcissistic; but for Butler it was not narcissism at all. Rejecting much of the institutionalized philosophy, science, and culture of his day, he was thrown upon his own intuitive perceptions for his raw material, and this he believed was the kind of material with which everyone should work. He regarded the dictates of the individual mind as nearly divine—what did not come from this source was most likely sham and affectation. He was like Thoreau and Emerson in his respect for the insights of his own individual moments, though Butler is more literal-minded than the two transcendentalists. It can also be said that keeping the notes was a kind of curative process for Butler himself. They surely helped to protect him from the pressure to conform and the pressure to give up his unrecognized and unrewarded activities, those activities that were motivated from so deep within him. The notes have a tremendous range, from passing thoughts on events of the day to philosophical meditations. Their dominant characteristic is the way in which, like his books, they challenge accepted views, turn traditional patterns upside down, scare, shock, and amuse. What a mental disciplining they are![25]

Modern readers no longer find the notes as exciting as readers in 1912 and the following years did.[26] Of course it is important to know the notes exactly as Butler wrote them, particularly for scholarly purposes, and we will be helped in this by the Breuer-Parcell project of putting them all into print, of which volume 1 has already appeared.[27] But it is hard for us to recapture the late Victorian or Edwardian state of mind, and the constant praise of compromise and of instinctive wisdom may strike the more rebellious among us as complacent. Several recent studies are so negative that they suggest that those who years ago admired these notes must have been mistaken.[28] Hans-Peter Breuer, in his lengthy introduction to the recent *The Note-Books of Samuel Butler, Volume I,* evaluates the notes in a way that would amuse Butler himself. The complex negatives and the "unconscious humor" (a term invented by Butler) reveal the opposite of what Breuer appears to say: for example, "This is not to say that his [Butler's] assessments were entirely without merit . . . his particular picques were not expressions of defensive jealousy only, but responses resting on not entirely inconsequential grounds"[29]—that is, in Breuer's opinion, apparently, the notes really are inconsequential.

To counter the negative response of recent readers one needs to remember the praise of earlier ones. Harold C. Goddard, for example, in a public address in the 1930s displayed a well-worn copy of *The Note-Books* and said that when he first discovered it, he felt stopped by an Ancient Mariner: he had to be dragged to his meals for days. "It is a masterpiece of wit and wisdom. It makes you laugh on every page, but then come back and discover it is not just a laughing matter. 'If a thing is funny' says Bernard Shaw [and Freud too] 'search it for a hidden truth.' "[30] Virginia Woolf observed that Butler was "amazingly fresh to the end of his life . . . life was a perpetual experiment which he was forever watching and manipulating and recording in his note-books; and if today we are less ambitious, less apt to be solemn and sentimental, and display without shame a keener appetite for happiness, we owe this largely to Butler's example."[31] His notebooks remain to this day a storehouse of joy and insight to anyone who will give them a chance.

Chapter Nine

The Rise to Fame and Summation

Having apparently failed successively to make much of a mark as a painter, as a satirist, as a scientist, as a literary critic and specialist in art, as a biographer, and as a Shakespeare critic, Butler developed the conviction that he was writing for the future (*Note-Books*, Shrewsbury Edition, 154). It is a vivid testimony to the deep toughness, even stubbornness, of his character that he stuck to this conviction in spite of his continuing failure to reach a wide audience or even to persuade publishers to bring out his books at their own risk. As already noted, he had failed in this, though trying hard, with his biography of his grandfather, his Homer translations, and also with everything else he wrote except *Erewhon Revisited* and the revision of *Erewhon*. Toward the end of his life he spent much time organizing his papers as though he knew that some day the world would take an interest in them. In a way, the soundness of his reliance on intuitive insights was confirmed when his popularity began to rise, although it did not rise all at once.

First Recognition

The decade or so after Butler's death gave only an inkling of the high reputation that he was to achieve later on. When he died in 1902, the obituaries that appeared were kind and considerate but not enthusiastic. R. A. Streatfeild, his literary executor, began the campaign to get him a wider hearing that was carried on during the next decade by his closest friends. An article by Streatfeild in the *Monthly Review*[1] described Butler's life and work in general terms. *The Way of All Flesh,* published in 1903, at first caused little excitement; among the leading journals few reviewed it at length, and the *Athenaeum*[2] described it as a failure. But in 1904 Arnold Bennett read it "with a real zest" and noted that "there is a vast amount of naked truth in the book."[3] Not until 1914 when Desmond MacCarthy published an article on "The

Author of *Erewhon*"[4] did anyone point out that all of Butler's works illustrate a general philosophy of life. He called Butler "a frank and consistent hedonist."

Butler became much better known with the publication of his notebooks (extracts in the *New Quarterly Review,* 1907–1910; book in 1912) that, combined with George Bernard Shaw's complimentary reference to him in the preface to *Major Barbara* (also 1907), succeeded in attracting attention. *The Note-Books* received a glowing front-page review in the London *Times Literary Supplement,*[5] the first time Butler had ever been given such attention. In 1908 several of his books were reissued. The annual *Erewhon* dinners, begun in 1908 by Marcus Hartog and Henry Festing Jones, continued until the outbreak of World War I. Among the speakers at these dinners were George Bernard Shaw, Edmund Gosse, Gilbert Cannan, Angus Birrell, and Desmond Mac-Carthy. Clutton-Brock's article in the London *Times Literary Supplement*[6] was a discussion of Butler that drew wide attention. In 1910, in a volume of essays commemorating the centenary of Darwin's birth, W. Bateson, professor of biology at Cambridge, called Butler "the most brilliant, and by far the most interesting of Darwin's opponents."[7] In his *Introduction to Biology and Other Papers*[8] A. D. Darbishire of the University of Edinburgh made wide use of Butler's biological theories and acknowledged his indebtedness. Another group of writers at this time began to take Butler seriously as a philosopher: Robert F. Rattray in *Mind*;[9] William Barry in the *Dublin Review*;[10] Gerold Pestalozzi in a German dissertation;[11] and May Sinclair in her *A Defence of Idealism.*[12]

Rising Popularity

The early enthusiasm, however, hardly forecast the upsurge in Butler's popularity that occurred after World War I when, Philip Henderson speculates, "the generation that suffered most from the war turned against their elders."[13] At this time *The Way of All Flesh* became very well known, and it has been widely read ever since. If Butler could have received a few cents for each copy that was sold in England, the United States, France, Germany, Italy, and many other countries he would have achieved a financial success far beyond his father's wildest hopes. In 1918 Orlo Williams wrote that Butler "is one of the few" of the writers immediately following the great Victorians "whose name is little likely to be forgotten by the generations to come," and that *The Way of All Flesh* "stands with the greatest English novels of the last century."[14] In 1919 Macmillan published Henry Festing Jones's two-volume *Memoir*[15] which contains an impressive collection of facts that have been used by all later writers on Butler, even those who see him very differently from the way Jones saw him. In retrospect, some recent critics feel that Butler's closest friend overwhelmed him with an outpouring of petty detail,[16] but if the effect of Jones's monumental study (979 closely packed pages) is at times trivial, this results more from Jones's rather unimaginative selection of material than from the realities of Butler's own existence, as Mrs. Charles Gogin, who had known Butler well, recognized on reading the book.[17]

If Butler was admired at first for his iconoclastic onslaught on Victorian complacency, his popularity was bound to fade when it became no longer the custom to downgrade the Victorians. But after a period of reassessment in the 1920s, sounder reasons for praising him began to emerge. In the United States Paul Elmer More inaugurated a more careful study of Butler in the *Unpartizan Review*,[18] finding a deep vein of poetry in Butler that he felt was unfortunately much overlaid and praising him for a "superbly clear and idiomatic English style." C. E. M. Joad's *Samuel Butler*[19] takes Butler's biological theories very seriously indeed and defends them well, and Louis and Madeleine Cazamian devoted careful attention to him in their history of English literature and in a study of the English novel.[20] M. P. Willcocks in *Between the Old World and the New*[21] says that "at bottom, Butler is a man of prodigious faith, as well as of reverence." Clara Stillman's *Samuel Butler, a Mid-Victorian Modern*[22] is primarily a study of Butler's ideas but does him an injustice by continually emphasizing his modernity, as though he were chiefly a spokesman for the age to come. Robert F. Rattray's *Samuel Butler: a Chronicle and an Introduction*[23] is a serious attempt to set Butler in his entirety before the reader. "The records of Butler," he says, "reveal a heart hungry to love and to be loved." In 1935 Herbert Davis remarked in an article on Butler in the *University of Toronto Quarterly*[24] that unfortunately Butler's reputation is still based on his excursions into literature and not upon the results of his "patient pursuit of knowledge."

Idolizing Ends

But in 1936 Butler's admirers, some of whom had overdone their admiration, received a sharp satiric blow from Malcolm Muggeridge's *A Study of Samuel Butler, the Earnest Atheist*. As Furbank points out in his *Samuel Butler, 1835–1902,* this work creates a fictional figure based on some of the facts of Butler's life and on the foolish idolatry he aroused in certain quarters, and then savagely destroys this fiction, leaving the real Butler relatively untouched. The author's use of the word *earnest* in his title reveals, Butler would have said, that his "attention was arrested by sincerity, as by something more or less unfamiliar to himself" (*Life and Habit,* 24). Muggeridge's study is a forerunner of Ralf Norrman's much more damaging analysis in *Samuel Butler and the Meaning of Chiasmus* and of the lukewarm and sometimes negative analyses in Daniel F. Howard and Hans-Peter Breuer.[25]

In 1938 Ernest A. Baker, in his *History of the English Novel,* called *The Way of All Flesh* "a very great novel" and said that it had had as potent an influence on the modern novel as that exercised by Flaubert, the Goncourts, de Maupassant, and Zola.[26] The most important books on Butler from the forties and fifties are those by P. N. Furbank and Philip Henderson; these books make use of sharp analysis and precise psychological deductions and are well worth study. One of Henderson's most valuable insights is that "Butler's scientific books were far more revolutionary than even he realized, for here he is on the verge of the whole vast subject of social psychology—a subject whose importance has only been recognized in our time."[27]

More recently a large amount of useful scholarly activity has annotated the Butler texts and provided more reliable readings. The most important of these activities is Daniel F. Howard's edition of *Ernest Pontifex, or the Way of All Flesh* (1964), an excellent edition going back to Butler's manuscripts and undoing the editorial work of Streatfeild. Useful too are Breuer and Howard's revival of the 1972 text of *Erewhon,* the publication of Butler's family letters edited by Arnold Silver (1962), of his letters to his sister May, and the attempt to get the entire notebooks into print.[28]

Valuable book-length studies of Butler in the 1980s are Thomas L. Jeffers's *Samuel Butler Revalued,* which relates Butler to time-honored British conservative traditions, and Ralf Norrman's *Samuel Butler and the Meaning of Chiasmus,* which attempts to use elaborate theorizing about the relationship between rhetorical devices and the personalities and outlooks of those who use them to explain Butler's work. Looking very closely at Butler's style, Norrman finds clues in its confusion of order, of beginning and end, of right and left, that he believes explain Butler's compulsiveness: it was not the urgency of what he had to say, this scholar maintains, that moved him onward so much as his unusual orientation and his style. This intriguing but distressing analysis differs from the attempt to see the father-son conflict that obviously dominated Butler's life as a crucial motivation of all his work and is not based on psychoanalytic insights. Norrman finds that Butler's thoughts, particularly as he gets older, often settle "into a number of well-worn grooves, and then rumble on inevitably, one well-known chiastic idea [an idea derived from changing the order AB into the order BA] suggesting another, until Butler has made his ritual tour of them all."[29] But what does this approach do for readers who enjoy Butler and even his repetitions? Butler, Norrman says, did not really want any solution to problems: "What he was after was not the solution, only the problem itself."[30] He sees Butler as a confirmed dualist, a lover of symmetry (his dualism and love of symmetry probably resulted from emotional starvation in childhood) and unable to take sides. This last inability led him to take a "cruel attitude to various kinds of victims throughout his writing."[31] Norrman says "whoever understands chiasmus will also understand Butler. . . . It is hardly an exaggeration to say that everything he observed went through a chiastic filter."[32] He admits that "many of these inversions are fairly witty and really do open the reader's eyes to things he may not have seen before."[33] But still he maintains that inverting all order was compulsive for Butler and finally disastrous to him. The experts in this kind of rhetorical analysis will have to appraise Norrman's achievement. In the meantime, most readers interested in literature will return to a consideration of Butler's ideas rather than move to such an exclusive emphasis on how he expressed them and on the biological intricacies of his brain.

Last Word

In *The Cradle of Erewhon* Joseph Jones wrote: "I am aware that whoever meddles with Butler is likely to start more hares than he can chase."[34] This observation succinctly suggests the problem faced by those who seek to evaluate the work of Samuel Butler. No matter what is said about him and backed up from the Butler texts, there are always unexpected hares springing out from statements elsewhere in those same texts that one cannot chase. This complexity results not only from Butler's belief in the ability of everything to convert into its opposite (as Norrman says), but also from his reliance on intuitive insights. Butler remains a thoughtful, chameleonlike, even (in his challenge to Victorian morality) satyrlike figure, ready and willing to entrap anyone who pontificates about him because he hates all pontification and all dogmatism, and is quite dogmatic about this himself. "Above all things," he writes, "let no unwary reader do me the injustice of believing in *me*. In that I write at all I am among the damned" (*Life and Habit*, 35).

But Butler would demand that we come to terms with him, no matter how difficult that may be. He had little patience with those who refuse to formulate or to think about their reactions. In *Shakespeare's Sonnets Reconsidered,* as we have seen, Butler had written about those who say "read the sonnets if you like, but do not go below their surface," "I do not write for these good people . . . I . . . pass them by at as wide a distance as I can" (100). His notebooks are in one sense his own extended struggle to understand his puzzling mind, a kind of self-conducted psychoanalysis.

Although not a romantic, Butler developed a strong reliance on grace above knowledge, intuition above reason, unconscious thoughts above conscious ones.[35] This reliance may in part have stemmed from the fact that he learned early in life, as the result of his traumatic but successful quarrel with his father, to rely on himself rather than on what the world around him seemed to be telling him. We can say that some of his insights are dead wrong, as such insights often are. Most grating is his scornful treatment of Goethe, who had more in common with him than he would ever know,[36] and Dante, and Beethoven. On the other hand, many of his intuitions were exactly right. In 1870, for just one example, he guessed that the *Three Fates* by Michelangelo in the Uffizi Gallery could not possibly be his, and this insight has been confirmed by recent scholarship.[37] Still, in spite of this "intuitionism" we are always reminded of Butler's sound common sense. He writes in his notebooks: "Reason is not the ultimate test of truth, nor is it the court of first instance. . . . Nevertheless, it is folly to appeal from reason to faith unless one is pretty sure of the verdict and, in most cases about which we dispute seriously, reason is as far as we need go" (*Note-Books,* Shrewsbury Edition, 334). Thomas Jeffers rightly points out how much this commonsense position owes to Butler's English predecessors of the eighteenth century, Locke, Hume, and Chesterfield.[38]

Our world believes above all in specialization, and we would thus affirm that Butler dabbled in too much to become really first-rate in anything. But an alternate view is fairer: he, again like Goethe, though with far less genius,[39] was one of the last "universal" men who tried in his life to realize what a human being is capable of. He never became a great painter, but his achievements in art were not negligible, as shown by his entries accepted in the Royal Academy Exhibits and his illustrations to *Alps and Sanctuaries;* he was not an experimental scientist but his scientific books explore philosophical questions still not decided; his satirical work continues to arouse debate, interest, and admiration, though it does not conform to the usual literary canon; his art criticism and research are flawed by quarrelsomeness, and his biography of his grandfather, though praised when it appeared, is now seldom looked at; his classical studies and translations and his study of Shakespeare's sonnets have also been neglected and not seriously evaluated; and his novel, though trail-breaking and powerful, is flawed by an ending far less powerfully written than the first half: but who else in recent memory has tried so much? In addition, he wrote music and poetry and himself played the piano. It was not sublime egotism that led him to do all this and to believe that he could achieve something in so many areas, but rather his profound faith in dropping his inhibitions, in refusing to defer to what authorities wanted, and in simply trying to do what his deeper self demanded that he do.

The enormous energy Butler poured into his books—"My books are to me much the most important thing in life. They in fact are me much more than anything else is."[40]—as earlier into his painting and later into his art research and music, demanded a great deal of him and did not leave him free to lead what others would call a normally successful life—earning money, raising a family, having a wide circle of friends—which he had no desire to do anyway. Recent publication of his family letters, however, and of more information, some of it suppressed by Jones in his endeavor to create an enfant terrible, shows a kindly, considerate man who went to extraordinary lengths not to hurt anyone's feelings, even his sisters' when they served him coffee for breakfast, knowing that he preferred tea.[41]

Butler was not kind or considerate, however, but tough when it came to combatting whatever he regarded as hypocrisy, sham, or affectation. And unfortunately, being so devoted to the idea that each individual should be true to his own insights, he was inordinately hard on absolutely anyone he suspected of self-serving deference to authority. This suspiciousness of others accounts for his overt rudeness to writers he regarded as sycophants.[42] Unfortunately, as the years went on and he became more and more enamored of his own ideas, he came to believe that more and more people fitted into this category. This belief led to his deep conviction that all those who rejected the idea of an inherited unconscious memory on which his *Life and Habit* theory was based must be hypocritically riding the coattails of Darwin's growing fame. He simply could not see that they were true to their own belief that there is no place in objective science for such psychological considerations. This blindness was the major damaging obsession of his life. Nevertheless, he went on with his work.

Butler's greatest gift as a writer is his clarity of expression, shown most admirably in the best of his notes. In an age that more and more admired purple prose—one thinks of the admiration for Ruskin, Pater, Stevenson—Butler was exceptional in his frontierlike insistance on direct, unadorned statement. One's joy in reading him has much to do with one's appreciation of this directness and forcefulness, each sentence saying exactly what it wants to say. This simplicity, though, does not mean that Butler, like some frontiersmen, avoided complexities or denied their presence; indeed, too often his direct attack landed him in trouble, as in the complexities it caused him to discover in Darwinism and later, by extension, in the whole social order and in religious faith. It led him, too, sometimes, and regretably, to an overarrogant self-consciousness, an impatience with others and their ideas, a too-great willingness to heap scorn and ridicule on people who often did not deserve them, and on ideas sometimes better and nearer the truth than he and his admirers could imagine. The dogmatism that hated dogma occasionally thus became a dogma itself.[43] But this trap did not catch Butler as often as his detractors believe. He did not always accept his own philosophy. He came near to becoming an existentialist, aware of the tragedy of existence.[44] His greatest defect, then, is that he did not go far enough in the direction so many of his insights pointed. He too often accepted a weakly comic world, a world of witticisms, of the burlesques that Overton, the narrator of *The Way of All Flesh,* wrote, a world that shortsightedly rejected so much that was happening in other greater worlds than its own.

Butler's *Erewhon,* one of his two best books, has the sterling quality of simplicity and directness and reveals his ability to use this directness to suggest a transformation of values in showing up the looking-glass Erewhonians who expose absurd European civilization by their often equally absurd habits and beliefs. *Erewhon* marks the beginning in the Victorian world of the awareness of cultural relativism that has been carried so much further by twentieth-century anthropologists and philosophers. It is sui generis; it cannot be fitted into any one category of satire, romance, or science fiction. This very fact gives it special life.

In *The Fair Haven* Butler grappled with material he did not yet fully control. Thus his critique of various levels of religion and irreligion lost balance, and the work stands there today capable of reflecting and refracting many confusing interpretations. By its very confusion of aim, which robs it of the satiric power its author thought he was achieving (see his "Preface to the Second Edition," *The Fair Haven,* xvii–xxii), it becomes a harbinger of Butler's ambiguous feelings about orthodox religion signaled later in his life by repeated assertions that he was a Broad Churchman though he remained unforgiving of the "hoax" of the Christian miracles that even Broad Churchmen must accept.

Life and Habit is Butler's most surprising book and the most paradoxical, never yet refuted or proved right because no one except possibly Jung has devised a way of dealing with the sort of haunting suggestions involved in the idea that instinct is an unconscious inherited memory. This suggestion may have originated in Butler's interest in music, since skillful performers must be as unconscious of most of what years of practice have taught them as we are of our digestive processes. It ties us to all our ancestors and creates a unified organic world, which, as Butler later saw, can be called the living god, thus for him solving the problem unsolved by the complexities of *The Fair Haven.* To Butler these insights to which he came with much excitement and which he elaborated throughout the rest of his life were profoundly meaningful, and indeed they are a Victorian prophecy of our own interest in and awareness of the unconscious as an important influence in our lives. But the scientific world of Butler's day could not deal with what he was saying, as even now it cannot effectively deal with Freud and Jung. Let it be noted, however, that to this day no one is quite sure what instinct is or how it is passed on from one generation to the next.

Butler's greatest achievement was his carefully wrought but not fully revised *The Way of All Flesh,* the novel that saw five generations of Englishmen through the eyes of Lamarckian-Darwinian evolution and mixed chance and purpose into a series of lives that were terribly botched and yet fulfilled. He provided an exposé of the Victorian domestic world or of any world that relies on conventionality and hypocrisy, which exposé should give the deathblow to all such worlds. At the same time, in his fumbling "hero" Ernest, Butler detailed what those not born to grace (as he conceived Towneley to be) can achieve for the future in becoming conscious of what life means—willing, as Jeffers points out,[45] to move from the contented island in the treetops of our simian forefathers and of the Towneleys out onto the doubtful savannahs of the future. In inventing a smug but often right-minded narrator for his complex tale Butler skillfully left his novel open to complex multiple meanings and created a masterpiece that is a forerunner of and template for many modern explorations of unorthodox life patterns.

Butler's three other books on evolution besides *Life and Habit* are quarrelsome and unnecessarily disrespectful to Darwin; they are also repetitious. But each has remarkably vivid passages, each is in part a joy to read because of the clever use of debating techniques and of clearcut, effective prose. In *Evolution, Old and New* Butler drew attention to the long development of evolutionary thinking before Darwin; he even claimed that, in spite of ironic denials, Buffon had firmly believed in the transmutation of species and in the formative effect of environment on organic development. In this claim, however, he understated the dramatic power of Darwin's perception that the struggle for survival is the sufficient and only cause of evolutionary development, a point Butler was never able to acknowledge or concede. In *Unconscious Memory* he restated his *Life and Habit* theory and expressed in argumentative, sometimes angry, rhetoric his annoyance that no one would even argue with him, though he saw signs that some biologists were actually adopting his views. In *Luck, or Cunning?* he once more defended his conviction that purposiveness extends throughout all organic life: Can we believe that a squirrel stores nuts in the fall merely by chance, not because he wants to survive the winter? Butler was afraid of the mindless universe of the scientific evolutionists: his arguments are so entertaining, so lucid, so forceful even, that it is sad that, like so much rationalizing, they finally fail to convince.

Butler's variegated other work is also a testimony to his energy and strength, if not always to his good sense. Surely he must have known that professional art historians would not accept his enthusiasm for the wood, terra cotta, and plaster statues in the North Italian sanctuaries as elaborated in *Ex Voto;* that the Shakespeareans would be shocked by his reading of the sonnets; and that no matter how interesting, even compelling his arguments, classicists would not agree that Nausicaa wrote the *Odyssey.* There must, it seems, be a carefully organized world of scholarship with precise rules about how everything is done and no patience for outsiders who use those rules in an inspired, amateurish way. But anyone occasionally annoyed by the stuffiness of the scholarly world must rejoice at the bravado of the gifted and inspired frontiersman who tries to invade the inner sanctuaries, even while understanding why he is not let in. As for Butler's *Life and Letters* of his grandfather, anyone trying to read its many pages today would agree that the aging Butler was far too idolatrous, wordy, and unselective in this enormous and tiresome undertaking.

The *Note-Books* and *Alps and Sanctuaries* are so informed by Butler's mischievous, thoughtful, questioning spirit as to rank with the best of their kind in spite of blemishes. Anyone who has read the eight volumes of the notebooks in the Chapin Library, many pages in Butler's clear flowing hand, will never forget the pleasure and enjoyment. There has not been another travel book like *Alps and Sanctuaries:* opinionated but tolerant, human in its anecdotes, expressing Butler's most relaxed acceptance of life along with his awareness of much that is to be hated and rejected. It is a good book to remember when thinking of its troubled, driven, inspired, and irrepressible author.

Notes and References

Chapter One

1. Wayne G. Hammond lists the recent studies of Butler (since about 1935) in "Samuel Butler: A Checklist of Works and Criticism," *Samuel Butler Newsletter* 3, nos. 1 and 2 (1980):13–24, 51–66, and 4, no. 1 (1981):6–20. The chief earlier bibliography is Stanley B. Harkness, *The Career of Samuel Butler, 1835–1902, a Bibliography* (London: Bodley Head, 1955).

2. Opposing explanations of Butler are found in such studies as Henry Festing Jones, *Samuel Butler, Author of Erewhon (1835–1902)—a Memoir* (London: Macmillan, 1919); Mrs. R. S. Garnett, *Samuel Butler and His Family Relations* (London and Toronto: J. M. Dent, 1926); Malcolm Muggeridge, *A Study of Samuel Butler, the Earnest Atheist* (London: G. P. Putnam, 1936); P. N. Furbank, *Samuel Butler, 1835–1902* (Cambridge: Cambridge Press, 1948); and Ralf Norrman, *Samuel Butler and the Meaning of Chiasmus* (London: Macmillan, 1986).

3. Philip Henderson called his study *Samuel Butler, the Incarnate Bachelor* (London: Cohen & West, 1953), the phrase having originated with the ladies at Heatherley's Art School (Jones, *Butler,* 1:140).

4. Jones, *Butler,* 1:212–13.

5. Page numbers given in the text in parentheses refer to the Shrewsbury Edition of *The Works of Samuel Butler,* ed. Henry Festing Jones and A. T. Bartholomew (London: Jonathan Cape, 1923–26), except for references to *The Way of All Flesh,* which are to *Ernest Pontifex, or The Way of All Flesh,* ed. Daniel F. Howard (Boston: Houghton Mifflin, 1964).

6. For example, Sister Mary Bernetta Quinn, "Ernest Pontifex as Antihero," *English Fiction in Transition* 5, no. 1 (1962):30–31.

7. Furbank, *Samuel Butler,* 22.

8. Editha and Richard Sterba, *Beethoven and His Nephew* (New York: Pantheon, 1954).

9. Butler's family background is given in Jones, *Butler,* 1:1–17.

10. In a note written in October 1883 Butler says: "I could publish my novel which is all ready for the press, and so keep myself before the public, but as long as my father lives how can I do this?" MS *Note-Books,* vol. 2, p. 8, Chapin Library, Williams College.

11. Norrman, *Samuel Butler and Chiasmus,* 34 and passim.

12. Jones, *Butler,* 1:20–21.

13. *The Family Letters of Samuel Butler,* ed. Arnold Silver, (Stanford, Calif.: Stanford University Press: 1962).

14. Garnett, *Samuel Butler and His Family Relations*.

15. Jerome Hamilton Buckley, *The Victorian Temper* (Cambridge, Mass.: Harvard University Press, 1951), 117–18.

16. Ruth Gounelas, "Samuel Butler's Cambridge Background and *Erewhon*," *English Literature in Transition* 24, no. 1 (1981):17–39.

17. Jones, *Butler*, 1:39.

18. Ibid., 60.

19. For another example of this see *Alps and Sanctuaries* (Shrewsbury Edition, 1924), 7.

20. Jones, *Butler*, 1:58.

21. "A Clergyman's Doubts," *Examiner*, 15 February 1879.

22. Jones, *Butler*, 1:59.

23. This idea is used in *The Fair Haven* and is hinted at in *Erewhon* (Shrewsbury Edition, 1923), 29.

24. Jones, *Butler*, 1: 61.

25. Silver, *Family Letters*, 74–75.

26. Ibid., 76.

27. Ibid.

28. Ibid., 79.

29. Ibid., 62.

30. Jones, *Butler*, 1:87.

31. Ibid., 37.

32. Ibid., 89–95.

33. Ibid., 71.

34. Ibid., 74.

35. Silver, *Family Letters*, 158.

36. Joseph Jones, *The Cradle of Erewhon: Samuel Butler in New Zealand* (Austin: University of Texas Press, 1959).

37. *Eagle*, vol. 2, 101, 149; vol. 3, 18.

38. Jones, *Butler*, 1:72, 73.

39. Jones, *Cradle*, 1.

40. See also Silver, *Family Letters*, 104.

41. Jones, *Cradle*, 79 and passim.

42. Robert B. Booth, *Five Years in New Zealand* (London: J. G. Hammond & Co., 1912), quoted in Jones, *Butler*, 1:87.

43. L. J. Kennaway, *Crusts* (London, 1874), quoted in Jones, *Cradle*, 52.

44. Jones, *Butler*, 1:96. See also Silver, *Family Letter*, 104–5.

45. Jones, *Butler*, 1:97.

46. Ibid., 98.

47. Ibid., 99.

48. Ibid., 100.

49. *Press*, 28 October 1863, quoted by Jones, *Cradle*, 202.

50. Jones, *Butler,* 2:284–87. But Ross Stuart in "Samuel Butler and Charles Paine Pauli: a Friendship Reconsidered," *English Literature in Transition* 28:145–61, speculates that Pauli gave Butler literary advice as well as friendship, and that the money Butler paid him could have been considered a retainer fee.

51. Jones, *Butler,* 1:115.

52. Ibid., 59, 117.

53. Ibid., 117.

54. Ibid., 118.

55. Ibid.

56. Ibid., 122.

57. Ibid., 123.

Chapter Two

1. Jones, *Butler,* 1:132–33.

2. *Ibid.,* 357.

3. *Samuel Butler and E. M. A. Savage, Letters, 1871–1885,* ed. Geoffrey Keynes and Brian Hill (London: Jonathan Cape, 1935).

4. Jones, *Butler,* 1:144.

5. Ibid., 224, 444–48.

6. Jones, *Butler,* 2:349–50.

7. Jones, *Butler,* 1:148–49.

8. Ibid., 154–55.

9. Gounelas, "Samuel Butler's Cambridge Background and *Erewhon,*" 22.

10. *Erewhon, or Over the Range* (London: Trübner, 1872). These original wordings are both given in notes 1 and 2 on p. 78 of the Hans-Peter Breuer and Daniel F. Howard edition of *Erewhon* (Newark: University of Delaware Press, 1981).

11. Jones, *Butler,* 2:330–31.

12. Breuer/Howard edition of *Erewhon,* 212.

13. Hans-Peter Breuer, "The Source of Morality in Butler's *Erewhon,*" *Victorian Studies* 16:317–28.

14. Herbert Sussman, *Victorians and the Machine* (Cambridge, Mass.: Harvard University Press, 1968).

15. William Paley, *Natural Theology* (1802); Joseph Butler, *Analogy of Religion* (1736).

16. Sussman, *Victorians and the Machine,* 138.

17. G. N. Sharma, "Butler's *Erewhon:* the Machine as Object and Symbol," *Samuel Butler Newsletter* 3, no. 1 (1980):3–12.

18. Ibid., 3.

19. *Athenaeum,* 20 April 1872, 492.

20. *British Quarterly Review* 56 (July 1872):137.

21. *Fortnightly Review* 17 (May 1872):609–10.

22. *Saturday Review* 20 April 1872, 507–8.

23. "The New Gulliver," *Spectator* (20 April 1972):492–94.

24. Jones, *Butler,* 1:156.

Chapter Three

1. This thesis is central to Thomas Lindon Jeffers, *Samuel Butler Revalued* (University Park: Pennsylvania State University Press, 1981) and Govind Narain Sharma, "Samuel Butler and Edmund Burke: a Comparative Study in British Conservatism," *Dalhousie Review* 53 (1973):5–29.

2. Norrman, *Samuel Butler and Chiasmus,* 150.

3. Jones, *Butler,* 1:175.

4. See, for example, a letter to Mr. Fleay, 24 March 1873, in which Butler explains that he hopes to make a row (Butler Collection, Chapin Library, Williams College).

5. This is the thesis of Ina Rae Hark, "Samuel Butler and the Gospel of No Gospel," *Samuel Butler Newsletter* 2 no. 1 (1979):10–23.

6. Philip Henry Gosse, *Omphalos* (London: J. Van Woorst, 1857). For a summary of the conflict between religion and science of the period see Edmund Gosse, *Father and Son* (New York: Charles Scribner's Sons, 1907), especially chapter 5, and Frank M. Turner, *Between Science and Religion: the Reaction to Scientific Naturalism in Late Victorian England* (New Haven: Yale University Press, 1974).

7. Professor William Ellery Leonard told me that he had heard James praise Butler, but I know of no written evidence that James had read him. In July 1894, however, Butler wrote a long note approving of James's contention (in an article in *Mind,* April 1884) that we do not cry because we are sad, but are sad because we cry (MS *Note-Books,* vol. 2, p. 77, Chapin Library, Williams College).

8. Jones, *Butler,* 1:182.

9. Ibid., 175.

10. *Academy,* 7 February 1874.

11. Jones, *Butler,* 1:186–87.

12. Silver, *Family Letters,* 158–59.

13. Jones, *Butler,* 1:216.

14. Silver, *Family Letters,* 161.

15. Morse Peckham makes a useful distinction between "propositions and implied assumptions which may be properly ascribed to a source in the *Origin,*" which he calls Darwinian, and those not so properly ascribed, which he calls "Darwinistic," "Darwinism and Darwinisticism," *Victorian Studies* 3 (1959):3–40. Butler is mostly Darwinian in these books when he analyzes the ambiguous language Darwin used in describing the variations his theory depends upon, and Darwinistic when he embarks on his unconscious-memory theory.

16. *Further Extracts from the Note-Books of Samuel Butler,* ed. A. T. Bartholomew (London: Jonathan Cape, 1934), 54.

17. Gertrude Himmelfarb, *Darwin and the Darwinian Revolution* (New York: Doubleday, 1962), 445, quoting J. Gray in *Nature* 173 (1954):227.

18. Basil Willey, *Darwin and Butler—Two Versions of Evolution* (London: Chatto, & Windus, 1960), 83.

19. Ibid., 47.

20. See, for example, Phyllis Greenacre, *The Quest for the Father* (New York: International Universities Press, 1963).

21. Phyllis Greenacre states that Butler's organic memory "might be compared very roughly with ideas of unconscious mental functioning, which had already been glimpsed but did not come into any usable theoretical form until Freud," ibid., 42.

22. Jones, *Butler,* 1:233.

23. Ibid., 242–43.

24. Ibid., 288.

25. Ibid., 264.

26. *Origin of Species* (London: 1876), 233. Quoted by Butler, *Life and Habit,* 197.

27. *Athenaeum,* 26 January 1878, 118–19.

28. *Contemporary Review* 32 (May 1878):406.

29. *Westminster Review* 109 (April 1878):240–41.

30. *Saturday Review* 45 (26 January 1878):119–21.

31. *Spectator,* 9 February 1878.

32. *Nature* 19 (27 March 1879):477–80.

Chapter Four

1. *Unconscious Memory* (Shrewsbury Edition, 1924), 10. The phrase is Darwin's own description of his account of the history of evolutionary theorizing. The account first appeared in the third edition of *The Origin.*

2. Basil Willey, among others, accepts Butler's analysis of Buffon in *Darwin and Butler—Two Versions of Evolution,* 78.

3. *Academy* 15 (17 May 1879):426–27.

4. *Nature* 20 (12 June 1879):141–44.

5. See Jones, *Butler* 2, appendix C, 446–67, for an account of this affair.

6. R. A. Copland, writing in *Notes and Queries* 24:23–24, reports that in the copy of *Erasmus Darwin* Butler gave to the British Museum he erased a note referring to the *Kosmos* article ("see *Kosmos,* February, 1879") that would indicate to the reader that the book was more than a mere translation. Would such a note, however, overcome the effect of Charles Darwin's preliminary notice, as Copland thinks it would? Still, one wonders why Butler erased it.

7. Jones, *Butler* 1:323.

8. *Athenaeum,* 31 January 1880.

9. For additional information on the misunderstanding unknown to Jones see *The Autobiography of Charles Darwin,* ed. Nora Barlow (New York: Harcourt, 1959).

10. Ibid., 186.

11. Ibid., 216.

12. Norrman, *Samuel Butler and Chiasmus,* 267.

13. For example, see Muggeridge, *A Study of Samuel Butler, the Earnest Atheist,* or Greenacre, *The Quest for the Father.*

14. Jones, *Butler* 1:332.

15. Karl Robert Edouard von Hartmann, *Philosophy of the Unconscious* (London: 1869). C. G. Jung in his *Psychology of the Unconscious* (New York: Dodd, Mead, 1931) finds "a deep psychological justification" for part of the von Hartmann view (198); but in *Psychological Types* (New York: Harcourt Brace, 1933) he says he is not "a frank adherent of the Hartmann philosophy" (209). Later, however, he links it with his "collective unconscious" in *The Integration of the Personality* (New York: Farrar & Rinehart, 1939), 52.

16. *Athenaeum,* 18 December 1880, 810.

17. *Nature* 22, (27 January 1881):285–87.

18. Jones, *Butler,* 1:349–50.

19. *Athenaeum,* 1 March 1884, 282–83.

20. *Athenaeum,* 8 March 1884, 312–13.

21. Jones, *Butler,* 1:404.

22. *Athenaeum,* 22 March 1884, 378–79.

23. In a letter in *Nature,* 12 August 1866.

24. *Athenaeum,* 22 January 1887, 131–32.

25. *Athenaeum,* 13 April 1887, quoted in Jones, *Butler,* 2:49.

26. *Academy* 30 (18 December 1886):413.

27. Jones, *Butler,* 1:384–85.

28. Howard, *The Correspondence of Samuel Butler with His Sister May,* 204.

29. Jones, *Butler,* 1:251.

30. Ibid., 334.

31. Ibid., 356.

Chapter Five

1. Jones, *Butler,* 1:202.

2. Ibid., 204.

3. Ibid., 205.

4. But Ross Stuart in "Samuel Butler and Charles Paine Pauli: a Friendship Reconsidered," in *English Literature in Transition* 28 (1985):145–61, speculates, without firm proof, that Pauli was "first and foremost" among the sympathetic collaborators Butler required to "stimulate his mind and

convince him of the reality of his ideas" (150), thus putting his influence ahead of the traditionally recognized influence of Miss Savage.

5. Jones, *Butler* 1:203.

6. Ibid., 391.

7. Ibid., 398.

8. Ibid., 206–7.

9. Margaret Ganz calls Overton Butler's "alter ego," which undermines the more intriguing and plausible idea that Butler is ironic about him and his ideas, even though he is obviously a good deal like the older Butler in his "existential composure," in "Samuel Butler: Ironic Abdication and the Way of the Unconscious," *English Literature in Transition* 28, no. 4 (1985):375, 370. Avrom Fleishman, however, agrees with me in saying that in Overton Butler reduces his mature self to an aesthetic object and throws ironic light on it, in *Figures of Autobiography* (Berkeley: University of California Press, 1983), 257–58.

10. Jones, *Butler,* 1: 208. Daniel F. Howard argues unpersuasively that Butler's mother inspired the portraits of both Christina and Alethea (see his introduction to his edition of *Ernest Pontifex, or The Way of All Flesh,* ix.) The page references to *The Way of All Flesh* in this chapter are to this edition, and not to the Shrewsbury Edition, which is used for all Butler's other books.

11. Jones, *Butler,* 1:390.

12. Ibid., 2:1. See also two sonnets, "Remorse," *Note-Books,* 424.

13. Howard, *Ernest Pontifex, or The Way of All Flesh,* vi.

14. Fleishman, *Figures of Autobiography,* 262.

15. W. C. Knoepflmacher, *Religious Humanism and the Victorian Novel: George Eliot, Walter Pater, and Samuel Butler* (Princeton: Princeton University Press, 1965), 270.

16. *The Correspondence of Samuel Butler and His Sister May,* ed. Daniel F. Howard (Berkeley: University of California Press, 1962), 65.

17. The original letter is given in Silver, *Family Letters of Samuel Butler,* 40–42.

18. Ibid., 12.

19. *Samuel Butler and Chiasmus,* 223. Norrman gives a rhetorical analysis of a passage from *The Way of All Flesh,* chapter 19, in which Overton defends George Pontifex.

20. Claude T. Bissell, "A Study of *The Way of All Flesh," Nineteenth Century Studies,* ed. Herbert Davis (Ithaca, N.Y.: Cornell University Press, 1940), 303.

21. Fleishman, *Figures of Autobiography,* 260. Daniel F. Howard changed the title back to the way it appears on Butler's MS to emphasize the individual Ernest Pontifex, but both Fleishman and Margaret Ganz (in "Samuel Butler: Ironic Abdication," 369) prefer the more general title used

by Streatfeild in the original edition. She says "The Way" can mean "road, manner, mode, or destiny," and "Flesh" can mean "humanity, physical, cellular, genetic unity, or fallibility."

22. Jones, *Butler,* 1:389–90.

23. John Henry Raleigh, "Victorian Morals and the Modern Novel," *Partizan Review* 25 (Spring 1958):241–64.

24. Fleishman, *Figures of Autobiography,* 267.

25. Margaret Ganz, "Samuel Butler: Ironic Abdication," 367.

26. Ibid., 372.

27. Knoepflmacher, *Religious Humanism,* 270.

28. Furbank makes a special point of this in his *Samuel Butler, 1835–1902.*

29. For example, by Daniel F. Howard in the introduction to his edition of *Ernest Pontifex, or The Way of All Flesh,* x, and by Sister Mary Bernetta Quinn, "Ernest Pontifex as Anti-hero," 30–31.

30. The thesis that Butler did not recognize the importance of art as Joyce did is developed in Ilse Dusoir Lind, *"The Way of All Flesh* and *A Portrait of the Artist as a Young Man:* a Comparison," *Victorian Newsletter* 9 (Spring 1956):7–10.

31. John B. Rosenman, "Evangelicism in *The Way of All Flesh,*" *College Language Association Journal* 26, no. 1 (1982):84.

32. Naseeb Shaheen, "Butler's Use of Scripture in *The Way of All Flesh,*" *Essays in Literature* 5 (1978):39–51.

33. Fleishman, *Figures of Autobiography,* 257–58.

34. Sister Rita Yeasted, "The Handelian Quality of Butler's *The Way of All Flesh,*" *Modern Language Studies* 9, no. 2 (1979):23–32. For more on Butler's love for Handel see Hans-Peter Breuer, "Samuel Butler and George Frederic Handel," *Dalhousie Review* 55 (1975):467–90.

35. On 2 August 1874 Butler wrote Miss Savage from Montreal, where he was trying to save the money he had invested in a Canadian company: "If I fail I shall have to write novels for my bread. I *will* too," Jones, *Butler,* 1:214.

36. Margaret Ganz, "Samuel Butler: Ironic Abdication," 384.

37. Ibid., 386.

38. Ibid., 381, 375.

Chapter Six

1. Carroll Wilson speculates in a note in the Chapin Library Butler Collection (Williams College, Williamstown, Massachusetts) that just before his death Butler made Streatfeild rather than Jones his literary executor because he knew that the former would be able to publish *The Way of All Flesh* immediately, whereas Jones, who was acquainted with Butler's sisters, would not.

2. Basil Willey calls these the "three great explosions . . . which rocked the fabric of Christendom and sent believers scuttling for shelter," *Darwin and Butler—Two Versions of Evolution,* 9.

3. For example, Daniel F. Howard, *"Erewhon* as a Victorian Document," *Samuel Butler Society Newsletter* 1, no. 2 (1978):7, 9; also Ina Rae Hark, *"The Fair Haven* and the Decline of Butler's Victorian Career," paper read at the MLA Annual Meeting, Chicago, 1977, p. 4.

4. Jones, *Butler,* 1:214.

5. Ibid., 2:49.

6. H. F. Jones, "Samuel Butler: A Sketch," *A First Year in Canterbury Settlement and Other Early Essays* (London: Jonathan Cape, 1923), lii.

7. Thomas L. Jeffers remarks that "Poor Butler wanted so much to be loved that he was grateful for the licks of an English terrier," *Samuel Butler Revalued* (University Park: Pennsylvania State University Press, 1981), 64, referring to a passage in Jones, *Butler,* 2:211. Philip Henderson quotes Desmond MacCarthy as saying of Butler: "His manner was that of a kind old gentleman, prepared to be a little shocked by any disregard of the proprieties. . . . He spoke softly and slowly, often with his head a little down, looking gravely over his spectacles and pouting his lips, with a delicate demureness so disarming that he was able to utter the most subversive sentiments without exciting more than a moment's astonishment" (the Samuel Butler number of *Life and Letters,* October 1931; *Butler, the Incarnate Bachelor,* 165).

8. Jones, *Butler,* 2:54.

9. In a note on 18 April 1893 Butler says that he chose "the fighting road rather than the hang-on-to-a-great-man road" and suffered accordingly, *Note-Books,* 381.

10. Jones, *Butler,* 1:145.

11. Furbank believes the desire for personal discoveries is characteristic of Butler, *Samuel Butler, 1835–1902,* 21.

12. *Spectator* 61 (4 August 1888):1065.

13. Passages like this give credence to Furbank's suggestion that Butler wanted to destroy science. He certainly did want to destroy pretense in science.

14. Jones, *Butler,* 2:73.

15. Ibid., 1:237.

16. Ibid., 2:81, 252.

17. Ibid., 2:198, 227.

18. *Spectator* 77 (21 November 1896):731.

19. *Athenaeum,* 24 October 1896, 555–56.

20. *Academy* 50 (28 November 1896):449.

21. Jones, *Butler,* 2:259.

Chapter Seven

1. Jones, *Butler,* 2:105.
2. Ibid., 121.
3. *Athenaeum,* 30 January and 20 February 1892. See Jones, *Butler,* 2:123–24.
4. Robert Graves, *Homer's Daughter* (London: Cassell, 1955), 9. In 1975 Ruth Hoppin wrote that Louise George Clubb had remarked at a symposium at the University of San Francisco that the *Odyssey* is a "woman's book" and had echoed Butler's belief that "The *Iliad* is a story about what men do. The *Odyssey* is the sort of thing women *think* men do . . ." (*Samuel Butler Society Newsletter* 1, no. 1 [Winter 1978]:9–13, from David Wallechinsky and Irving Wallace, *People's Almanac* [Garden City, N.Y.: Doubleday 1975]).
5. Jones, *Butler,* 2:172.
6. Ibid., 207–8.
7. *The Iliad of Homer,* trans. Ennis Rees (Indianapolis: Bobbs-Merrill, 1963), vii.
8. *The Odyssey of Homer,* trans. T. E. Shaw (New York: Oxford University Press, 1932), 'iv.
9. Richard Lattimore, for example, says: "And did he [Homer] write both *Iliad* and *Odyssey?* This is not a soluble problem and it is not, to me, a very interesting one; it is the work, not the man or men who composed the work, which is interesting" (*The Iliad of Homer* [Chicago: University of Chicago Press, 1951], 29).
10. Alison Booth, "The Author of *The Authoress of the Odyssey:* Samuel Butler as a Paterian Critic," *Studies in English Literature* 25, no. 4 (Autumn 1985):865, 867.
11. Ibid., 865.
12. Ibid., 868.
13. Ibid., 879.
14. Ibid., 877.
15. Ibid., 882.
16. *Saturday Review* 84 (4 December 1897):625–27.
17. *Notes and Queries* 12, 8th ser. (4 December 1897):458–59.
18. Jones, *Butler,* 2:207.
19. Ibid., 105.
20. They were reprinted for the Classics Club by Walter J. Black, New York, 1942, for mass mail-order circulation. Saul Bellow wrote in the *New Yorker* articles (out of which came his book *To Jerusalem and Back*) of reading the *Iliad* and the *Odyssey* in Butler's translation (see *Samuel Butler Society Newsletter* 1, no. 4 (Fall 1978):10.
21. *Academy* 55 (26 November 1898):328–29.
22. *Athenaeum,* 12 November 1898, 668.
23. *Notes and Queries* 2, 9th ser. (19 November 1898):419.

24. Jones, *Butler*, 2:311.

25. Ibid., 231.

26. Hans-Peter Breuer, "A Reconsideration of Samuel Butler's *Shakespeare's Sonnets Reconsidered*," *Dalhousie Review* 57 (Autumn 1977):513.

27. Ross Stuart, "Samuel Butler and Charles Paine Pauli: a Friendship Reconsidered," *English Literature in Transition* 28:159.

28. Muggeridge, *A Study of Samuel Butler, the Earnest Atheist*, 260–61.

29. Edward Dowden, *Shakespeare—A Critical Study of His Mind and Art* (London: Kegan Paul, Trench & Co., 1889), 394–402.

30. Donald E. Stanford, "Robert Bridges and Samuel Butler on Shakespeare's Sonnets: An Exchange of Letters," *Shakespeare Quarterly* 22 (1971):329.

31. Rolf-Dietrich Keil says that "In jahrzehntelanger Mosaikarbeit hat Sir Denys Bray schliesslich die Bestätigung seiner Hypothese gefunden" ("In decades-long mosaic work Sir Demys Bray finally found the proof of his hypothesis"), that metrical and verbal links can be used to reestablish the order of the sonnets. I do not believe, however, that Shakespeare scholars have agreed about this. *Shakespeare, die Sonnette* (Düsseldorf-Köln: Eugen Diederichs Verlag, 1939), 7.

32. Stanford, "An Exchange of Letters," 333, 335.

33. *Academy* 58 (6 January 1900):15.

34. *Notes and Queries*, 18 November 1988.

Chapter Eight

1. Jones, *Butler*, 2:393.

2. Ibid., 396.

3. Ibid., 251, 331.

4. Ibid., 339.

5. *Samuel Butler's Notebooks*, ed. Geoffrey Keynes and Brian Hill (New York: E. P. Dutton, 1951), 46.

6. Jones, *Butler*, 2:339–41.

7. Furbank takes special note of this.

8. This resemblance is discussed in detail by Adam J. Bisanz, "The 'Grand Inquisitor' Motif in Samuel Butler's *Erewhon Revisited*," *Revue de Litterature Comparée* 47:369–83.

9. *Further Extracts from the Note-Books of Samuel Butler*, 26.

10. Fleishman, *Figures of Autobiography*, 265.

11. Ibid., 264.

12. *Erewhon, or Over the Range*, ed. Breuer and Howard.

13. Ibid., 16.

14. Ibid., 19.

15. Ibid., 24.

16. The many differences between the 1872 text and the 1901 text were first pointed out in my "Samuel Butler's Revisions of *Erewhon*," *Papers of the Bibliographical Society of America* 38 (1944):22–38.

17. *Erewhon*, ed. Breuer and Howard, 20.

18. Ibid., 30.

19. H. F. Jones, preface to the first edition, *The Note-Books of Samuel Butler* (London: Jonathan Cape, 1926), xxxvii–xliii, and Hans-Peter Breuer's "General Note on the Text," *The Note-Books of Samuel Butler, Volume I (1874–1883)* (Lanham, Md.: University Press of America, 1984), xi–xv, are the best sources of information about Butler's notebooks. See also the "Introduction" to *Further Extracts from the Note-Books of Samuel Butler*, ed. Bartholomew.

20. *The Note-Books*, ed. Breuer xl.

21. *The Note-Books*, ed. H. F. Jones, xxxix.

22. See a fuller discussion of the reception in the next chapter. Also see my "Samuel Butler's Rise to Fame," *Publications of the Modern Language Association* 57 (September 1943):875–76.

23. The following page references are all to this reprinting, with a few additions, of the 1912 edition.

24. *The Note-Books*, ed. Breuer, 56; page references inserted parenthetically in the following text refer to this edition.

25. Three other selections from Butler's notebooks were published after the 1926 reprinting of Jones's selections in the Shrewsbury Edition: *Butleriana*, ed. A. T. Bartholomew (London: Nonesuch Press, 1932); *Further Extracts from the Note-Books of Samuel Butler*; and *Samuel Butler's Note-Books*, ed. Geoffrey Keynes and Brian Hill (London: Jonathan Cape, 1951).

26. Hans-Peter Breuer, for example, says that in 1976 Jonathan Cape, which had once "loyally brought out Butler items was now unwilling to reissue its own Selections from the Note-Books, out of print for some time," "Butler on a Balance of Considerations," *Samuel Butler Newsletter* 2, no. 2, (1979):41.

27. From a statement on p. v of *The Note-Books of Samuel Butler, Volume I*, (1874–1883), ed. Breuer.

28. This conclusion is forced upon one by Hans-Peter Breuer's introduction to *The Note-Books of Samuel Butler*, ed. Breuer, and by many comments in Norrman, *Samuel Butler and Chiasmus*.

29. *The Note-Books*, ed. Breuer, 12.

30. From a privately owned typescript.

31. Virginia Woolf, *Contemporary Writers* (London: Hogarth Press, 1965), 31, from a review published 20 July 1916.

Chapter Nine

1. *Monthly Review*, September 1902.

2. *Athenaeum*, no. 3944 (30 May 1903):683.

3. *The Journal of Arnold Bennett* (New York: Viking Press, 1932) 194–95.

4. Desmond MacCarthy, *Independent Review* 3 (September, 1914):527–38.

5. *Times* (London) *Literary Supplement,* 5 December 1912, no. 569.

6. Ibid., 9 October 1908, no. 352.

7. W. Bateson, "Heredity and Variation in Modern Lights," *Darwin and Modern Science* (Cambridge: Cambridge University Press, 1910), 88.

8. A. D. Darbishire, *An Introduction to Biology and Other Papers* (London: 1917).

9. Robert F. Rattray in *Mind* (July 1914) n.s. 23:371–85.

10. William Barry in *Dublin Review* 155 (October 1914):322–44.

11. Gerald Pestalozzi, *Samuel Butler der Jüngere. Versuch einer Darstellung seiner Gedankenwelt* (Zürich: J. Ruegg, 1914).

12. May Sinclair, *A Defence of Idealism* (London: Macmillan, 1917).

13. Henderson, *Butler, the Incarnate Bachelor,* 132.

14. Orlo Williams, *Modern English Writers* (London: 1918), 327, 330.

15. H. F. Jones, *Samuel Butler, Author of Erewhon (1835–1902)—A Memoir* (London: Macmillan, 1919).

16. For example, Jeffers, *Samuel Butler Revalued,* 5, states that Jones's biography "both consummated the posthumous glorification and began the inevitable disillusionment."

17. Letter in the Chapin Library Butler Collection, from Mrs. Gogin to Robert F. Rattray, May 1935.

18. Paul Elmer More in *Unpartizan Review* 15 (January 1921):20–42; reprinted in *Shelburne Essays,* 11th ser. (Boston: Houghton Mifflin, 1921), 167–99.

19. C. E. M. Joad, *Samuel Butler* (London: L. Parsons, 1924).

20. Louis and Madeleine Cazamian, *Histoire de la Litterature Anglaise* (Paris: Hachette, 1924) and *Le Roman et les Idées en Angleterre* (Strasbourg: Librairie Istra, 1923).

21. M. P. Willcocks, *Between The Old World and The New* (London: G. Allen and Unwin, 1925).

22. Clara Stillman, *Samuel Butler, a Mid-Victorian Modern* (London: Viking Press, 1932).

23. Robert F. Rattray, *Samuel Butler* (London: Duckworth, 1935).

24. Herbert Davis, in *University of Toronto Quarterly* 5 (October 1935):21–36.

25. See, for example, the introduction to *Erewhon, or Over the Range* (1981).

26. Ernest A. Baker, *The History of the English Novel,* vol. 10 (London: 1939), 267, 246.

27. Henderson, *Butler, the Incarnate Bachelor,* 123.

28. The first volume in this project has already appeared: *The Note-Books of Samuel Butler, Volume I, 1874–1883*, ed. Breuer. Roger E. Parsell will also do editorial work in this project.

29. Ralf Norrman, *Samuel Butler and the Meaning of Chiasmus* (London: Macmillan, 1986), 223.

30. Ibid., 261.

31. Ibid., 120.

32. Ibid., 4.

33. Ibid., 39.

34. Joseph Jones, *The Cradle of Erewhon* (Austin: University of Texas Press, 1959), viii.

35. Gerald Levin in "Shaw, Butler, and Kant," *Philological Quarterly* 52:142–56, analyzes Butler's use of reason and instinct and relates it to both Kant and Shaw.

36. Goethe also strove to be an artist, unsuccessfully; wrote on scientific subjects and quarreled with those who opposed him; and wrote a bildungsroman. But Goethe was too securely established by his greatness as a lyric poet and too unaware of unconscious humor to be acceptable to the Ishmaelitish Butler who regarded him as one of the seven humbugs of Christianity.

37. *The Correspondence of Samuel Butler and His Sister May*, 50.

38. This is a major thesis of *Samuel Butler Revalued*.

39. Concerning genius, Butler remarked (*Evolution Old and New*, 341) "Mr. Allen has said that I am a man of genius. . . . I have been subjected to a good deal of obloquy and misrepresentation at one time or another, but this passage by Mr. Allen is the only one I have seen that has made me seriously uneasy about the prospects of my literary reputation."

40. *The Correspondence of Samuel Butler with His Sister May*, 116.

41. Henderson, *Butler, the Incarnate Bachelor*, 226.

42. For example, when Emery Walker introduced Butler to William Morris one evening and Morris said, "Good evening, Mr. Butler. I am much pleased to make your acquaintance. I have read your books with interest," Butler rudely replied, using exactly the same words except for the name, and each of them then went on his way (Ibid., 206).

43. Ina Rae Hark makes this point in "Samuel Butler and the Gospel of No Gospel," *Samuel Butler Newsletter* 2, no. 1:10–24.

44. U. C. Knoepflmacher develops this idea in *Laughter and Despair: Readings in Ten Novels of the Victorian Era* (Berkeley: University of California Press, 1971).

45. Jeffers, *Samuel Butler Revalued*, 108.

Selected Bibliography

PRIMARY SOURCES

Complete Works

The Works of Samuel Butler. Edited by Henry Festing Jones and A. T. Bartholomew. Shrewsbury edition. 20 vols. London: Jonathan Cape, 1923–26. The individual volumes of this definitive edition will not be listed in this bibliography, but (with the exception of *The Way of All Flesh,* see below) are referred to throughout the text by title and page number.

Novel

The Way of All Flesh. London: Grant Richards, 1903.
Ernest Pontifex, or The Way of All Flesh. Edited by Daniel F. Howard. Boston: Houghton Mifflin Co., 1964. This text is derived directly from Butler's manuscript and undoes the editorial work of R. A. Streatfeild, who prepared the novel for publication after Butler's death. Howard believes that "the unretouched text is in a livelier, more informal style, full of colloquialisms that Butler naturally used" and that many changes that Streatfeild made had the effect of hiding some of Butler's meaning. References to *The Way of All Flesh* in this book are to this more reliable edition.

Satirical Romances

Erewhon, or Over the Range. London: Trübner, 1872.
Erewhon, or Over the Range. Edited by Hans-Peter Breuer and Daniel F. Howard. Newark: University of Delaware Press, 1981. This edition reestablishes the 1872 text but also includes in an appendix all the changes that Butler made in 1901 so that the careful student can separate the two versions of the work.
Erewhon Revisited. London: Grant Richards, 1901.

Writings on Evolution

"Darwin among the Machines," signed "Cellarius." *Press* (Christchurch, New Zealand), 13 June 1863.
"Darwin on Species," letters signed "A. M." *Press,* 21 February, 18 March, 22 June 1863.

"Darwin on the Origin of Species: a Dialogue." *Press,* 20 December 1862.
"The Deadlock in Darwinism." *Universal Review,* April, May, June, 1890.
Evolution, Old and New. London: Hardwicke & Bogue, 1879.
Life and Habit. London: Trübner, 1878 (issued December 1877).
Luck, or Cunning? London: Trübner, 1887 (issued 1886).
"Lucubratio Ebria." *Press,* 29 July 1865.
Unconscious Memory. London: David Bogue, 1880.

Notebooks

Butleriana. Edited by A. T. Bartholomew. London: Nonesuch Press, 1932.
Further Extracts from the Note-Books of Samuel Butler. Edited by A. T.
    Bartholomew. London: Jonathan Cape, 1934.
The Note-Books of Samuel Butler. Edited by Henry Festing Jones. London:
    Fifield, 1912.
"The Note-Books." *New Quarterly,* nos. 1–4, 6, 9, 10 (1907–1910).
The Note-Books of Samuel Butler, Volume I (1874–1883). Edited by Hans-
    Peter Breuer. Lanham, Md.: University Press of America, 1984. This
    is the first volume of the complete edition of Samuel Butler's manuscript
    notebooks (1874–1902) and for the first time makes all his notes
    available exactly as he wrote them.
Samuel Butler's Note Books. Edited by Geoffrey Keynes and Brian Hill.
    London: Jonathan Cape, 1951. This text prints selected notes chrono-
    logically with editing only to correct slips of the pen, but it is by no
    means a complete transcription of all the notes.

Religious Writings

"A Clergyman's Doubts." Letters in the *Examiner,* 15, 22 February; 1, 8,
    15, 22, 29 March; 5, 19 April; 10, 17 May; 14, 18 June, 1879.
"The Evidence for the Resurrection of Jesus Christ as Given by the Four
    Evangelists, Critically Examined." Privately printed pamphlet, 1865.
The Fair Haven. London: Trübner, 1973.
"Free Thinking and Plain Speaking." *Examiner,* 20 December 1873.
"God the Known and God the Unknown." *Examiner,* 24, 31 May; 14, 21,
    28 June; 12, 19, 26 July, 1879.
"Precaution in Free Thought." *Reasoner,* 1 August 1865.

Travel

Alps and Sanctuaries. London: David Bogue, 1882.
"Our Emigrant," signed "Cellarius." *Eagle* 2 (1860):101, 3 (1861):18.
A First Year in Canterbury Settlement. London: Longman, Green, Longman,
    Roberts & Green, 1863.
"Our Tour." *Eagle* 1, no. 5 (Easter Term 1895): 241–55.

Biography

The Life and Letters of Dr. Samuel Butler. London: John Murray, 1896.

Translations

The Iliad of Homer. London: Longmans, 1898.
The Odyssey Rendered into English Prose. London: Longmans, 1900.

Art

"Art in the Valley of the Saas." *Universal Review,* November 1890.
"L'Affaire Holbein-Rippel." *Universal Review,* November 1889.
Ex Voto. Londoon: Trübner, 1888.
"A Medieval Girl School." *Universal Review,* December 1889.
"A Sculptor and a Shrine." *Universal Review,* November 1889.

Literary Criticism

The Authoress of the Odyssey. London: Longmans, 1897.
Shakespeare's Sonnets Reconsidered and in Part Rearranged. London: Longmans, 1899.

Essays

Collected Essays by Samuel Butler. Edited by Henry Festing Jones and A. T. Bartholomew. Vols. 18 and 19 of *The Shrewsbury Edition of the Works of Samuel Butler.* London: Jonathan Cape, 1925. These volumes reprint the 1904 collection of Butler's essays, "The Humour of Homer," and twelve additional pieces.
Essays on Life, Art, and Science. London: Grant Richards, 1904.

Poetry

Narcissus. Words of the Choruses, 1887. Privately printed.
"Not on Sad Stygian Shore." *Athenaeum,* 6 January 1902.
"A Psalm of Montreal." *Spectator,* 18 May 1878.
Seven Sonnets and a Psalm of Montreal. Cambridge, 1904. Privately printed.

Music

Gavottes, Minuets, Fugues, etc. (with Henry Festing Jones). London: Novello, Ewer & Co., 1885.
Narcissus (with Henry Festing Jones). London: Weeks, 1888.
Ulysses (with Henry Festing Jones). London: Weeks, 1904.

Letters

The Correspondence of Samuel Butler and His Sister May. Edited by Daniel
F. Howard. Berkeley: University of California Press, 1962.
The Family Letters of Samuel Butler. Edited by Arnold Silver. Stanford, Calif.:
Stanford University Press, 1962.
Samuel Butler and E. M. A. Savage, Letters 1871–1885. Edited by Geoffrey
Keynes and Brian Hill. London: Jonathan Cape, 1935.

SECONDARY SOURCES

Bibliographies

Hammond, Wayne G. "Samuel Butler" A Checklist of Works and Criticism." *Samuel Butler Newsletter* 3, nos. 1, 2 (1980); 4:1 (1981). This
bibliography corrects errors in Harkness's 1955 work and adds many
items to it. See introductory note in 3, no. 1, 13–15.
Harkness, Stanley B. *The Career of Samuel Butler (1835–1902): A Bibliography.* London: Bodley Head, 1955. Numerous errors and omissions,
but at its time the most complete listing of Butler material.
Howard, Daniel F. "Samuel Butler." In *Victorian Fiction: A Second Guide
to Research,* edited by George H. Ford. New York: Modern Language
Association, 1978. A review of Butler research, 1964–74.

Critical Studies

Bekker, W. G. *An Historical and Critical Review of Samuel Butler's Literary
Works.* Rotterdam: Nijgh & Van Ditmar, 1925. A serious attempt to
find unity and value in Butler's work.
Brassington, A. C. *Samuel Butler in Canterbury: The Predestined Choice.*
Christchurch, New Zealand: Pegasus Press, 1972. More information
about Butler's New Zealand days.
Cannan, Gilbert. *Samuel Butler, a Critical Study.* London: M. Seeker, 1915.
The first book-length study of Samuel Butler.
Farrington, B. *Samuel Butler and the Odyssey.* London: Jonathan Cape, 1929.
Argues for acceptance of Butler's Homeric theories.
Fort, Joseph. *Samuel Butler, L'écrivain: Étude d'un Style.* Bordeaux: J. Bière,
1935. Concludes that although Butler used words cleverly, he lacked a
genuine style.
Furbank, P. N. *Samuel Butler, 1835–1902.* Cambridge: Cambridge University
Press, 1948. Thoughtful study that corrects some of Muggeridge's
distortions but argues that Butler's ego stood in his way and kept him
from real achievement.
Garnett, R. S. *Samuel Butler and His Family Relations.* London and Toronto:
J. M. Dent, 1926. An attempt to demonstrate that Butler misrepresented
his family in *The Way of All Flesh.*

Greenacre, Phyllis. *The Quest for the Father.* New York: International Universities Press, 1963. A Freud Anniversary Lecture studying Butler's relation with his father and with Charles Darwin in an attempt to understand the creative individual.

Harris, John F. *Samuel Butler, Author of Erewhon.* London: G. Richards, 1916. Early appreciative study, not so partisan as Gilbert Cannan's.

Henderson, Philip. *Samuel Butler, the Incarnate Bachelor.* London: Cohen & West, 1953. The best recent biography, but pays little attention to Butler's ideas.

Jeffers, Thomas L. *Samuel Butler Revalued.* University Park: Pennsylvania State University Press, 1981. Relates Butler to the conservative English thinkers of the eighteenth century. Thoughtful and sensitive analysis.

Joad, C. E. M. *Samuel Butler, 1835–1902.* London: L. Parsons, 1924. Enthusiastic account of Butler's biological theories.

Jones, Henry Festing. *Samuel Butler, Author of Erewhon (1835–1902), A Memoir.* London: Macmillan, 1919. Storehouse of biographical information, but not notable for objective character portrayal.

Jones, Joseph Jay. *The Cradle of Erewhon: Samuel Butler in New Zealand.* Austin: University of Texas Press, 1959. Some valuable new sidelights on Butler's years in New Zealand.

Maling, Peter Bromley. *Samuel Butler at Mesopotamia.* Wellington, New Zealand: Government Printer, 1906. New information about Butler's sheep ranch.

Muggeridge, Malcolm. *A Study of Samuel Butler, the Earnest Atheist.* London: G. P. Putnam, 1936. A damaging caricature of Butler, directed more at his admirers than at him.

Pestalozzi, Gerold. *Samuel Butler der Jüngere. Versuch einer Darstellung seiner Gedankenwelt.* Zürich: Universität Zürich, 1914. Discusses the ways in which Butler's creative career carries out ideas expressed in *Erewhon.*

Norrman, Ralf. *Samuel Butler and the Meaning of Chiasmus.* London: Macmillan, 1986. A technical analysis of the ways Butler's tendency to invert the order *A B* into the order *B A* affected all his thinking.

Stillman, Clara G. *Samuel Butler, a Mid-Victorian Modern.* New York: Viking Press, 1932. One of the best general discussions of Butler.

Willey, Basil. *Darwin and Butler—Two Versions of Evolution.* London: Chatto & Windus, 1960. Strongly suggests that the issues Butler raised are not dead, though Willey rejects Butler's *Life and Habit* theory.

Parts of Books

Bateson, W. *Darwin and Modern Science.* Cambridge: Cambridge University Press, 1910. First scientific discussion to pay close attention to Butler's *Life and Habit* theory.

Bissell, Clyde T. "A Study of *The Way of All Flesh.*" In *Nineteenth Century Studies,* edited by Herbert Davis. Ithaca, N.Y.: Cornell University Press, 1940. The novel interpreted in the light of Butler's theory of evolution.

Buckley, Jerome Hamilton. *Season of Youth: The Bildungsroman from Dickens to Golding.* Cambridge: Harvard University Press, 1974. Fits *The Way of All Flesh* into the long tradition of novels about growing up.

Cazamian, Madeleine L. *Le Roman et les Idées en Angleterre, L'influence de la Science, 1860–1890.* Strasbourg: Librarie Istra, 1923. Sees Butler as a product of his time.

Coveney, Peter. *The Image of Childhood: The Individual and Society: A Study of the Theme in English Literature.* Baltimore: Penguin, 1967. Takes Butler's account of Ernest Pontifex's childhood very seriously as an authentic image of childhood.

Fleishman, Avrom. *Figures of Autobiography.* Berkeley: University of California Press, 1983. Insightful discussion of *The Way of All Flesh* as a veiled autobiography.

———. "Personal Myth: Three Victorian Autobiographers, Mill, Gissing, Butler." In *Approaches to Victorian Autobiography,* edited by George P. Landow. Oxford: Ohio University Press, 1978. Puts Butler's novel in a well-established tradition of Victorian self-revelation.

Irvine, William. *The Universe of G. B. S.* New York: Whittlesey House, 1949. Many interesting comments on Butler's influence on Shaw.

Knoepflmacher, U. C. *Laughter and Despair: Readings in Ten Novels of the Victorian Era.* Berkeley: University of California Press, 1971. Butler achieved a new kind of outcome in *The Way of All Flesh:* not despair, and not quite laughter.

———. *Religious Humanism and the Victorian Novel: George Eliot, Walter Pater, and Samuel Butler.* Princeton: Princeton University Press, 1965. Butler accepts the hedonism Pater evaded but rejects the compromises of Eliot and Arnold. His novel is a parody of its own search. Butler "was too shrewd to believe in his own philosophy, but he was too faithful to question his 'dream.' "

Routh, H. V. *Towards the Twentieth Century.* New York: Macmillan, 1937. Links Butler with Nietzsche and Bergson for his attempt to adapt science to humanism, saying he failed because he was not a gifted writer.

Sussman, Herbert L. *Victorians and the Machine.* Cambridge: Harvard University Press, 1968. Explores the paradoxes in Butler's interest in Darwinism and his discovery that it tends to convert organisms into machines.

Turner, Frank M. *Between Science and Religion: the Reaction to Scientific Naturalism in Late Victorian England.* New Haven: Yale University Press, 1974. Discusses Butler in relation to many other attempts of his time to bridge the gap between science and religion.

Zabel, Morton D. *Craft and Character in Modern Fiction.* New York: Viking, 1957. Praises *The Way of All Flesh* for its extraordinary power.

Articles

Bisanz, Adam J. "Samuel Butler: A Literary Venture into Atheism and Beyond." *Orbis Literarum* 29 (1974):316–37. Thoughtful analysis by a European scholar: Butler was "tough minded" in his addiction to facts but "tender minded" in his need for religious belief. Under his mercurial eloquence lies a sincere pursuit of truth.

Booth, Alison. "The Author of *The Authoress of the Odyssey:* Samuel Butler as a Paterian Critic." *Studies in English Literature* 24, no. 4 (Autumn 1985):865–83. In his Homeric studies, like Higgs in *Erewhon,* Butler discovers a lost civilization and presents it as a criticism of contemporary life.

Breuer, Hans-Peter. "A Reconsideration of Samuel Butler's *Shakespeare's Sonnets Reconsidered." Dalhousie Review* 57 (Autumn 1977):507–24. Butler's approach is flawed because he disregarded the "making" aspect of the sonnets. Butler is a man of ideas, insensitive to the connotative quality of poetry.

———. "Samuel Butler and George Frederic Handel." *Dalhousie Review* 55 (Autumn 1975):467–90. Butler disliked Bach and Beethoven because he distrusted all professionalism and eschewed a wilderness of counterpoint: Handel's music remained linked to common experience. He did not understand orchestral music.

———. "Samuel Butler's 'The Book of the Machines' and the Argument from Design." *Modern Philology* 72 (May 1975):365–83. Either machines are a new form of life or living beings are machines. Traces the influence of Paley and Bishop Butler on Samuel Butler's thought. Argues that Butler's contribution was the assertion of purpose in evolution, not neo-Lamarckianism.

Ganz, Margaret. "Samuel Butler: Ironic Abdication and the Way to the Unconscious." *English Literature in Transition* 28, no. 4 (1985):366–94. Butler "anticipates our modern perception of uncertainty and contradiction at the heart of experience." His "ironic enterprise assumes the primacy of the unconscious."

Holt, Lee Elbert. "Samuel Butler and His Victorian Critics." *Journal of English Literary History* 8 (June 1941):146–59. Summarizes and evaluates the Victorian reviews of Butler's publications.

———. "Samuel Butler's Rise to Fame." *Publications of the Modern Language Association* 57 (3) (September 1942):867–78. Traces the response to Butler after 1900 that led to his becoming well known and widely read.

————. "Samuel Butler's Revisions of *Erewhon.*" *Papers of the Bibliographical Society of America* 38 (1944):22–38. Examines in detail the changes made in 1901 in the text of *Erewhon.*

————. "The Note-Books of Samuel Butler." *Publications of the Modern Language Association* 60, no. 4 (December 1945):1165–79. Tracks down the elaborate editorial work on the *Note-Books* of Henry Festing Jones by comparing his edition with the manuscript text in the Chapin Library.

Howard, Daniel F. "The Critical Significance of Autobiography in *The Way of All Flesh.*" *Victorian Newsletter* 17 (Spring 1960):1–14. Links Butler's quarrels with his father with the writing of the novel.

Knoepflmacher, U. C. "Ishmael or Anti-hero? The Division of Self in *The Way of All Flesh.*" *English Fiction in Transition* 4, no. 3 (1961):28–35. Analysis of the points of view from which the novel is written.

Levin, Gerald. "Shaw, Butler, and Kant." *Philological Quarterly* 52 (January 1973):142–56. Like other post-Kantian romantics, Butler failed to separate reason from intuition; Shaw also was an intuitionist.

Marshall, William H. "*The Way of All Flesh:* the Dual Function of Edward Overton." *Studies in Literature and Language* 4, no. 4 (Winter 1963):583–90. Analysis of Butler's narrator as both commentator on and participator in the action.

Pauly, Philip J. "Samuel Butler and His Darwinian Critics." *Victorian Studies* 25, no. 2 (Winter 1982):661–80. Butler's ideas that instincts were inherited habits and that intelligence was an important factor in evolution were common in the 1870s: Butler's most significant activity was "his attack on the belief that there was a 'Darwinian consensus.'"

Sharma, G. N. "Samuel Butler and Edmund Burke: A Comparative Study in English Conservatism." *Dalhousie Review* 53 (Spring 1973):5–29. Relates Butler's thought to the long conservative trend in England, particularly to Burke. Butler's concerns were primarily moral, not political: he asked fundamental questions about the nature of man.

Yeasted, Sister Rita. "The Handelian Quality of *The Way of All Flesh.*" *Modern Language Studies* 9, no. 2 (1979):23–32. The musical metaphor is essential to understanding the novel. Handel regains for Butler the balance that his age had lost, but Ernest and Overton cut themselves off from life itself.

Index

POCKET IN FRONT